Assessment in Counseling:
Understanding Why People Do What They Do

By
Stan E. DeKoven

Assessment in Counseling

ISBN# 978- 1-61529-005-5

For information on reordering please contact:

Vision Publishing
Ramona, CA 92065
1-800-9-VISION
www.visionpublishingservices.com

Table of Contents

Acknowledgements

I would like to thank three students and a professional colleague for their encouragement in this endeavor. Carolyn Scott, M.A., Dr. Nathaniel Hayes, and Dr. Jason Guerrero have encouraged me to put this material into somewhat of a coherent form. May God bless them and you as you develop into highly skilled ministers for the healing of the nations, and the restoring of the breach.

Introduction

When most students approach a course on psychological assessment, they do so with natural trepidation. Questions occur about the need for such tools. Are they really helpful? Can't we just "trust the Holy Spirit"? Well, we certainly do need the Holy Spirit's guidance when counseling someone. However, it is also helpful to gather as much information as possible regarding the client, before treatment begins. Many young counselors make serious mistakes in counseling people due to a lack of clear understanding of individuals, couples or groups real problems.

Before counseling begins, especially Family Counseling, it is essential that a thorough assessment of the presenting problem occurs. To assess a family is often highly more complicated than an individual assessment, since you are looking at the combined psychologies of at least two separate individuals that are inextricably linked by blood, culture, history, shared environment, etc. Further, all family units share roles, have myths to protect, have their own verbal and non verbal communication, etc.

Though complex, good assessment is quite possible. It includes components of individual assessment and branches out to areas of communication, beliefs, personal development, and family of origin dynamics within the life cycle, etc. Thus, it takes specific skills of observation mixed with scientific processes to develop clear pictures and patterns of family pathology, along with family strengths which will give guidance for the counseling process.

In this book, you will be tasked with grasping an overview of psychological measurements, and through the teaching provided in the comprehensive seminar which accompanies this book.

Each student will be given appropriate measurement tools for self assessment and other assessment tools that they will need to become proficient in. Students need to experience evaluation from both sides of the table, that is, all students must be familiar with the process of assessment from the counselors view and the counselees. Thus, conducting assessments will be a part of the repertoire of a proficient counselor.

This course will **not** make a student an expert at assessment. This is a beginning, and true skill at assessment will come as the student learns his/her skill through practice, practice, practice.

What is Assessment?

Assessment is nothing more than the gathering of facts, information that, when skillfully combined into a coherent whole can provide a clear picture of an individual, circumstance or situation. In the field of counseling, assessment is the utilization of the man made and God given (yourself, His gifts) tools to arrive at a diagnosis of the problem(s) of a person or family, so intervention or treatment can begin.

What Assessment is Not

Assessment of needs, though vital in terms of insight and understanding of individual needs or differences, is not a substitute for compassion, clinical skill, or integrity. Each tool that you will learn to use is but one piece of information about a member of God's precious creation. Humans are wonderfully complex, and truly the whole person is greater then the sum of the parts that we gather in our assessment process.

This Book

This introductory text was written to provide to the student an overview of assessment both psychological and psychosocial. It is broken down into four distinct but inseparable sections.

In the first section, you will find a brief overview of assessment and its application to clinical setting. Secondly, you will review the various types of measurement tools available in the general field(s) of psychology. Section three asks and answers (pay special attention, since exam questions will be written based upon this information) general and frequently asked questions regarding testing. You will find this most helpful. Section four reveals practical wisdom regarding administering tests, and provides sample tools (which may be different than your instructor has) for your information.

" Judge a man by his questions
rather than his answers."
Voltaire

Stan E. DeKoven

Section 1
Assessment and Clinical Application

Theories and Application of Counseling Assessment

The objective of this book is to provide the prospective counselor, psychotherapist, or clinical researcher with the rudimentary assessment skills necessary to begin an internship involving the utilization of standardized measures and objective tests of personality. Included in this volume will be:

The Importance of God in Assessments

Before any physician can help his patient, he must know what the problem is. How silly it would be for a person, having symptoms requiring a physician's care, when encountering the physician at the doctors' office, and asked to share the problem which brought the patient to the physician, states emphatically "I am too embarrassed to share it." The physician assures the patient that all shared will be confidential, and that regardless the problem, he will do all to assist them. Again, the patient states emphatically, "I just do not feel like telling you." Eventually, of course, the physician, in hopeless despair, will have to dismiss the potential patient, and will be able to provide no help to the suffering saint.

In a similar manner, the counselor who has a client who insists you guess what their problems are will have great difficulty helping the person in need. Thus, the counselor must ask questions in order to find out what the area of need might be. These questions must be presented in a professional, empathic manner, with respect and generally gentleness. Since most people come for counseling because they are in distress, we need not add to their distress.

In fact, it takes a significant amount of relevant information to determine what a person's problem may be. As a Christian Counselor, we dare not leave God out of the equation. That is, we as believers' recognize that the Lord is actively interested in assisting people to come into the fullness of their Godly identity. Thus, we rely on the work of the Holy Spirit in the believers life, along with insights that the Holy Spirit can bring, along with various spiritual disciplines to assist us in the assessment process.

For example, we know that the gifts of the Holy Spirit are readily available to counselors who are sensitive to the Spirit. Especially important are the gifts of discernment of spirits, the word of knowledge, word of wisdom. For the well trained counselor, these spiritual endowments are invaluable in determining why a person is struggling with an area of difficulty in their lives. Further, as we pray for a client, God can speak to us as care givers about the needs of the client, in ways that will defy logic but no doubt bring clarification to the needs presented.

God's Position on Man's Condition

In Jeremiah 17:9, the condition of man's heart is depicted as deceitful and sick. Most people who come for counseling do not need to be reminded that this universal condition without Christ is common to all, though eradicated in the spirit by the blood of Jesus. In fact, Jeremiah 17:10 clearly states that God says He knows the heart and how to deal with it. Thus, as believers we are partakers of this ability of God through the Holy Spirit who lives within us. God desires to help us understand the motivation and intentions of our hearts, and sensitive counselors, aware of the dual condition of man (with continued tendency towards self-deception and wickedness, e.g. Generational sin, and righteousness in Christ) work to assist a man or woman understand their heart and hopefully overcome their difficulties.

God is intimately involved in the life of every believer. Counselors need to rely on prayer, God's word, the gifts God provides, including a counselors natural wisdom and intuition to understand the dynamics of human behavior and individual dynamics of a person or family.

Definitions

It is often helpful to define an issue or problem as a first step in solving it. This is true in the process of assessment. Here are some important definitions of words relating to the assessment of people.

First, we might ask ourselves "what is normal"? Normal is defined in different ways. For instance, the medical definition is simply one who has no clearly defined diseased state or condition. That does not mean that a person is necessarily in the best of health, just disease free.

From a psychological view point, the psychosocial model states that a normal person is one who is effectively coping within a social setting. Thus, if a person has an area of sin in their life (such as homosexuality) but is "adjusting to their chosen lifestyle" they would be considered normal, even healthy. Of course, as Christian counselors, we would not see things in a similar way.

From a spiritual viewpoint, the needs of man or normal behavior are determined by Biblical standards found in the Word of God.

One area of assessment in the counseling process is the evaluation of personality. Personality is defined as the attitudes, habits, beliefs, and emotions developed by childhood experience over time of growth, in combination with the innate characteristics of an individual (temperament). Further, psychological disorders and diagnosis speak of what psychiatrists and psychologists use to classify and communicate with other professionals what the environment has done to an individual (to cause the symptoms). These symptoms are often classified in a Diagnostic and Statistics manual, such as the DSM-IV R, the latest version used in the field of psychology and psychiatry. Through this manual and the system developed by the American Psychiatric Association, psychopathology is determined. Psychopathology is the inability to cope due to maladaptive learning, negative reinforcement, family dynamics, personal choices, physiology or spiritual issues.

Of course, when one looks at the definition of normal or abnormal, the worldview of the person making the definition makes a major difference. For example, the ability to cope and behavior that satisfies oneself, which is the common definition of the psychological community, could be interpreted as a bank robber who loves his job! This definition would not be acceptable in any Christian circle. Thus, we must define normal from God's perspective, though the average person may fall well short of achieving His will. God's definition would no doubt include "Loving God with a whole heart, loving ones neighbor as oneself, being holy as He is holy, etc. thus, normal from God's viewpoint can only be achieved through Christ, by His grace, and is progressive in the life of every believer.

Dr. Bruce Narramore's 5 - Stage Model for the Development of Psychological Problems

Dr. Bruce Narramore,[1] a psychologist in California, has developed a very useful step by step understanding of how problems develop. This is useful in the assessment of needs, and very helpful in treatment goal planning. He elucidates five steps, with the following examples:

- Most people develop problems, often called psychopathology, due to a traumatic event or circumstance. Situations happen, caused by the imperfect world we live in, or by imperfect parents, etc. One person's trauma may not be another's, which can be seen in the wide gamut of individual differences found in people. The traumatic event or circumstance causes...
- Anxiety, often manifested as guilt, comes from the traumatic events. Anxiety is psychological or emotional pain. When emotional pain becomes too great for a person to bare, psychological defenses are triggered to help the person survive. These defenses are for our protection, and include:
  a. Projection – we see our defects in others instead of ourselves.
  b. Rationalization – we start making justifications for ourselves.
  c. Intellectualization – substitution of intellectual concerns for dangerous ideas and impulses.
  d. Undoing – attempt to cancel previous action.
  e. Reaction formation – acting opposite of what is unconsciously true.

---

[1] S. Bruce Narramore, and John Carter, Integration of Psychology and Theology, Zondervan Publishers, 1979

f. Ambivalence – preventing needed changes by constantly proposing why not's, or yes buts.

g. Displacement – attaching to a neutral object feelings that were really felt or generated towards someone or something else.

h. Identification – defense against feeling powerless, where a client identifies with strength of others.

i. Suppression – forcing of threatening desires or thoughts from awareness (I cannot believe I did that, so I didn't).

j. Sublimation – unacceptable drive channeled into socially acceptable activity (workaholic).

k. Acting out – expressions of unconscious emotional conflict by overt behavior – to avoid dealing with internal conflict.

As long as defenses work, people tend to be adjusted, coping with their life reality. However, when defenses stop working all together, or sufficiently to cause greater pain, symptoms will likely develop. These can include:

- Behavior – inappropriate acting out as in substance abuse, eating disorders, etc., affective – in emotional areas such as panic attacks, depression, bipolar disorder, etc., or cognitive – obsessive/compulsive thoughts, paranoid thinking or even psychotic thought processes like schizophrenia.

When symptoms become pervasive, they can hamper functioning and the growth of a person. This is called the:

- Limitation in the range of experience, (of the patient), thus psychopathology develops...the person becomes unable to work, play, function, etc.

When a client begins to experience this limitation in the range of normal and healthy experience, the ability to function, is when they usually seek help. The counselors' goals then focus on:

The alleviation of the anxiety and guilt triggering the defenses, followed by the resolution of the various traumas experienced.

With God's help, the healing process is then initiated.

Levels of Assessment

There are various levels of assessment, corresponding to the level of expertise of the counselor. A rule of thumb is this…never counsel above your level of education or experience. To do so is unethical, and may be harmful. For our discussion, there are three levels of assessment and subsequent counseling. They are:

Peer counseling, characterized by the following elements:

- Communication of empathy, warmth and respect.
- Asking questions about feelings or thoughts.
- Probing questions to help the client to talk about problems.
- 1-3 hours of time are required at this level.
- This level of assessment looks to provide a basic level of understanding of the clients needs and desires, and will help the client to
- Find the hurt and empathize with them.

The second level of assessment is that of Clinical pastoral

21

counseling. Added to the elements stated above, the trained pastoral or Christian counselor might add:

- Minor psychological testing, such as a Firo-B or DISC profile or the like.
- Take an extensive client history.
- Request input from other professionals or people of strong influence in the client's life, such as a social worker might do.

The third level of assessment is called the advanced professional level, which would include much of the above but would probably add:

- Significant psychological testing by:
- Trained professional in counseling, psychiatry, psychology, marriage and family counseling or social work, with a minimum of a master's or doctoral degree.

Again, the goal of any or all three levels is the same; "define the problem".

Summary of Steps: When the Process Begins

I have been asked on many occasions, when does the assessment process begin? Well, from my perspective, it begins with the first contact, whether by phone or in person. All assessment begins with observation, and recognition that it is the person you must get to know to help them, not their pathology (the person is not a symptom or a disease!).

Thus, the assessment process begins with the phone call. For example, if the wife calls due to distress with her husbands' drinking behavior, I immediately note that the problem is the wife's. That is, the person in distress is the wife, and treatment (including and beginning with assessment) will begin no doubt with the wife. I would make note of this basic observation, even though it starts before the beginning of counseling. Further, I will:

- Make notes of my conversation and observations, since I cannot trust my memory in all cases. Thus, I will write a simple statement in the client's own words of what the problem is...since that is the problem from the clients view. Following this, generally beginning at the first actual appointment, I will attempt to
- Obtain a good history on the client, as it relates to the stated problem. The fact is, people repeat significant patterns of behavior and thinking. These patterns, when discovered, should be noted and followed through on. Further, in some cases a more thorough evaluative exam will be given, with the hope of answering the following:
    1. General appearance: well dressed, immaculate?
    2. Do they look their stated age?
    3. Demeanor? Tense, suspicious, angry, etc...?
    4. Condition of their clothes?
- When warranted, I may conduct further assessment with various psychological tests, some of which are discussed in the sections to follow.
- Taken together, these bits of information add up to a complete picture of the client's needs. Thus, the counselor will need to gather as much information as possible and is useful, review the information, and pray over the information, asking for guidance and revelation from the Holy Spirit.

Hopefully, the whole picture will begin to take form. From there:

- Make a short, summary report expressing the counselor's impressions about the needs of the client. Make this report in descriptive or diagnostic terms, which will be helpful in the counseling process. From there, once the counselor
- Begins to put together all that has been learned into a picture of the client; uniting things like heredity factors, environmental factors, basic personality and temperament, stages of development and defense mechanisms, a clearer picture forms. Thus, you begin to answer the important question; how did the client come to this condition?

This forms the foundation for treatment goals and planning, which forms the foundation of the treatment process.

"I had six honest serving men who taught me all they knew; their names were Where and What and When, and Why and How and Who.' Kipling

The Assessment Interview

The assessment interview is a method of collecting information regardless of its purpose, form or content. It is probably the single most important means of data collection. Without interview data, psychological testing can be misleading and meaningless. Just as the physician seeks information to obtain a diagnosis and the lawyer seeks from his client information that may be legal evidence, the therapist seeks to obtain information to help reach a diagnosis and to check the validity of test results. The nature of the information may consist of a specific event, conscious or unconscious attitudes, overt and covert moral values, habits in recreation, ethical choices or feelings.

Therapists will want to assess the nature of the client's problem, relevant personal and family history, history of the problem, client's level of adjustment and the client's strengths. Techniques will vary from therapist to therapist. Some tools, such as *intake forms, life history questionnaire or one of the normally developed structured interviews, such as the Diagnostic Interview Schedule (DIS) or the Structured Clinical Interview for the *DSM-IV*[2] and (SCID).

Information may be given by the client very openly or freely, or it may be given with great reluctance, or not at all. Information obtained may take a casual ten minutes, an hour of intimate discussion or may take months of interviewing. The client may be doing his best to cooperate or doing his best to mislead the therapist. The information given may be given accurately or with conscious or unconscious distortion.

The therapist must maintain a healthy skepticism about the *reliability* and *validity* of any information and be constantly aware of possible error and distortion. *Error* can be caused by a number of reasons. The client may have a faulty memory, the memory may be distorted unconsciously, or he may be deliberately trying to mislead the therapist. Interviewer bias is also a consideration. The interviewer may allow first

---

[2] Italicized words or phrases are to be defined by the student as part of their course requirements.

impressions to bias later judgments, may consider a client more competent or mentally healthy than they actually are if they're friendly and warm, or may allow physical attractiveness to affect their judgments.

There are assets and limitations to both the structured and unstructured interviews. The unstructured is a person-centered approach, which allows one to focus on the individual and idiosyncratic factors. Rapport can be rapidly developed and client self-exploration can be encouraged. Hopefully, a trusting relationship develops between the client and therapist, which will assist them or perform and reveal themselves on the psychological tests. The greatest difficulty with the structured interview is the interviewer bias as previously mentioned. In emergency situation, the unstructured interview is the practical choice because decisions need to be made rapidly and test taking and interviews overlook the richness of the client, his idiosyncrasies and his unique characteristics may go unnoticed. Rapport may be lacking between the client and therapist, and personal information may be withheld. Structured interviews are very efficient and cost effective and the results allow comparing one case or population to another.

The assessment interview is an important method of data collecting and has an advantage over psychological testing in that the therapist can always check his own interpretation of the data. For instance, the therapist can ask for clarification in cases of inconsistency and in cases of ambiguity, he can ask about meaning. This is especially helpful when counseling an individual from a different culture.

The therapist's interviewing style will vary from therapist to therapist depending on his theoretical orientation, personal preferences and practicality. Interview questions will vary depending on the client's age, education, degree of cooperation, the presenting problem, or psychosis.

Success of an interview depends on the attitude which has been expressed and by what was said or done. Goals of the interview will be achieved if the client feels accepted or understood, feels the therapist is warm and sincere, feels the therapist has a genuine interest or a positive regard for him.

Checklists and intake forms are used by a therapist to obtain an overall picture of the client. There are many good examples to choose from or a form can be designed to specifically carry you smoothly through the interview process. General areas on your interview form might include:

1. History of the Problem (description, onset, intensity, and duration, previous treatment, attempts to solve, formal treatment, change in frequency, and antecedents and consequences).
2. Family background (socioeconomic level, parents' occupations, emotional/medical history, married/separated/divorced, family constellation, cultural background, parents' current health, family relationships, urban/rural upbringing).
3. Personal History

   a. Infancy Problem (developmental milestones, family atmosphere, amount of contact with parents, early medical history, toilet training).
   b. Early and Middle Childhood (adjustment to school, academic achievement, hobbies/activities/interests, peer relationships, relationships with parents, important life changes).
   c. Adolescence (all areas in early and middle

childhood, presence of acting out such as legal, drugs, sexual, early dating, reaction to puberty).
d. Early and Middle (career/occupational, inter-personal relationships, satisfaction with life goals, hobbies/interests/activities, marriage, medical/ emotional history, relationship with parents, economic stability).
e. Late Adulthood (medical history, ego integrity, reaction to declining abilities, economic stability).
f. Miscellaneous (self-concept likes/dislikes, what is your happiest/saddest memory, earliest memory, fears/somatic concerns, headaches, stomach aches, events that create happiness/sadness, recurring/ noteworthy dreams, etc.).

"When we remember we are all mad, the mysteries disappear and life stands explained." Mark Twain

Psychological Evaluations and Report Writing

The psychological report is the end product of the therapist's assessment. All of the collected data is put into a functional format, explaining to the client in a clear and relevant manner the therapist's conclusions in a useful way to help the client solve problems and make decisions.

The style of a report will vary with the therapist depending on his training. There are three general report writing styles – literary, clinical, and training. The literary style is creative, uses every day language, dramatic, but is often imprecise and prone to exaggeration. The clinical approach focuses on pathological dimensions of a person – the abnormal features, defenses, reactions to stress, dynamics involved in mal-adjustment, and it provides information about areas in need of change and alerts the therapist to potential difficulties. It also tends to be one-sided, omitting the person's strengths and tends to be an unrealistic view of the client. The scientific approach is more academic; it looks at and describes test findings in an objective, factual manner. It is often not respected by those of other disciplines because it is distant, cold and overly objective. Ideally, in actual clinical practices, therapists draw from all three approaches and effective report writing will integrate all three styles, effectively using the assets of each style. The result of the therapist report should be accuracy, clarity, integration, readability, usefulness and validity.

The format for a psychological report will vary with the therapist, but every report should include old information as well as new information. Old information should include identifying information (name, birth date), reason for referral and relevant history. New information should include assessment results, impressions, summary/conclusions, and recommendations. A suggested outline would be as follows:

Name:
Date of Birth:
Date of Examination:
I.   Referral Question
II.   Evaluation Procedures
III.   Behavioral Observations
IV.   Relevant History
V.   Test Results
VI.   Impressions and Interpretation
VII.   Recommendation

The referral question is a brief description of the client and the general reason for evaluating the client. A brief description of the nature of the problem should be included. An initial focus of the report and the types of issues to be addressed will be presented. The purpose for testing should be included, such as intellectual evaluation, assessment of the nature and extent of brain damage, or personal insight regarding difficulties with interpersonal relationships.

The evaluation procedure is simply a list of tests used and does not include the results. List the full test names and the abbreviations. The date of when the exam was taken and the length of time it took should be included for legal evaluations and other occasions in which precise details are important. If a clinical interview or *mental status exam* was given, include them here with the date and time required to take the exam.

Behavior observations can provide insight into the client's problem. Relevant observations include physical appearance, degree of cooperativeness and behavior toward the task and examiner. Note any contradictions, like a person who appears disheveled but has a high level of verbal fluency and an excellent vocabulary. It's also important to include the client's attitude to the test, if he had a good night's rest, if there's any use of medications or is there a situational crisis. Behavior observations should serve to develop some insight about the person or demonstrate his uniqueness.

A relevant history should include aspects of the person's background that are relevant to the problem and to the interpretation of the test results, if the problem and the test results are put into the proper context. The end product should include a good history of the problem, important life events, family dynamics, work history, personal interest, daily activity, and past and present interpersonal relationships. Begin with a brief summary of the client's general background including sex, age, family constellation, education, health, and restatement of the problem. Areas which can then be included and expanded on, according to its relevance to the problem can include description of parents and their status, atmosphere of family, recollections relevant from each stage of childhood, medical history, and organic impairment.

Test results do not need test scores unless they are for legal purposes or a professional will be reading the report. List intelligence tests first. Include *Verbal I.Q., Performance I.Q.,* and *Full Scale I.Q.* with sub-tests and scaled scores for the *Wechsler scales.* Follow with the *Bender* results, then the *MMPI* with the validity scales first, followed by scales from the highest to the lowest. Refer to the MMPI results by the *T scores* and not the raw scores. The Rorschach drawings can be summarized.

Impressions and interpretations are the main body of the report and is in the form of a hypothesis. Discuss the material by the different topics rather than test by test for a more integrated presentation. All information will be based on test data, relevant to the client's self-concept, emotional difficulties, overt behavior, family background, school problems, medical disorders, or interpersonal conflicts. The intellectual abilities are usually addressed first. Educational goals can also be included. Conflicts should be addressed – hostility, sexuality, or difficulties with dependency.

Recommendations are the practical part of the report. It is the suggested steps clients can take in order to solve their problems. Recommendations should be clear, practical and obtainable. The therapist must understand the nature of the problem, prescribe the best alternatives for remediation, and the resources available in the community to meet goals to solve the problem. Be specific in the recommendations and follow up to see if action has been taken or if your report has been filed and forgotten.

Overview of Clinical Assessment

Over the years, there has been extensive criticism and resistance to the use of psychological testing. Criticisms have included invasion of privacy, cultural bias, use of tests in inappropriate contexts, and the continued use of tests that are inadequately validated. Criticism has been the cause for the decrease in the use of traditional tests. Another reason for the decrease is the availability of alternative methods of assessment that are more specific, objective and observable.

Outcomes of scoring have been found to vary according to the relationship between the examiner and the client. Children scored higher when the child knew the examiner. Enhanced rapport with older children involving verbal reinforcement and friendly conversation also shows an increase in scoring. Disapproving remarks, such as, "I thought you could do better" resulted in significantly lower scores. Also, black students who were verbally praised by black examiners had significantly higher test scores.

The client's emotional state should be taken into consideration as to whether to administer the test. Assess the degree of motivation and his overall level of anxiety. Situational emotional states may significantly lower the test results and rescheduling the test may be the best alternative.

The most controversial issue regarding testing is their use with ethnic minorities. Critics state the tests are heavily biased in favor of and reflect the values of the white middle class society. They argue the test cannot adequately access the intelligence or personality of the minority group. The problems are complicated and far from being resolved. Several suggestions have been considered, including developing different and more adequate criterion measures. Another consideration is to increase access to educational and career opportunities. The therapist must remember the test scores are neither valid nor invalid, but can help to give some direction of treatment.

Selecting which psychological test to administer to a client is going to vary with the therapist's training, experience, personal preference, and familiarity with relevant literature. Example of testing can include the *Beck Depression Inventory* to assess depressed clients, the *McGill Pain Questionnaire*, the MMPI, and the *Illness Behavior Questionnaire* to pain patients. *Computer-Assisted Assessments* have become available over the past 20 years and have risen in popularity and have a number of advantages. Computers save valuable time, improve test reliability, reduce possible test bias and reduce consumer cost. Some controversies include untested validity because truthfulness decreases when the test is done on the computer and the use of the tests by unqualified people. The American Psychological Association established guidelines in 1986 yet 19% of the programs are being sold to the general public.

"What is the purpose of an examination—to find out what you know or what you don't know." Unknown

Psychological Testing : An Overview

There are several types of measurement tools available for

the Christian counselor. The primary types are described here.

Measures of Achievement

Achievement tests are tests which measure an individual's accomplishment or learning which has resulted from a relatively controlled condition and which is related to a particular subject or task. Probably everyone has had some direct experience with achievement tests: Remember those spelling and arithmetic tests in grammar school and final exams in college? They are examples of achievement tests.

Achievement Tests vs. Ability Tests

Most descriptions of achievement tests include a discussion of the differences between achievement and ability tests (i.e., tests of general intelligence, multiple and special abilities). Briefly, the primary differences between these two major types of tests can be summarized as follows:

Achievement test items are generally related to formal, specific, standardized, and recent learning which occurred in a controlled situation (e.g., a classroom). In contrast, ability tests tap broader areas of knowledge which are less the result of formal, specific and/or antecedent learning experiences and more the result of various and cumulative uncontrolled learning experiences. Because achievement tests are related to explicit learning situations, achievement test items are generally direct measures of what the test is assessing, while ability tests are indirect measures (i.e., the ability being the relationship between achievement tests and specific learning conditions, performance on achievement tests is more affected (improved) by coaching than is performance on tests of general intelligence or ability).

While ability tests, like aptitude tests, are generally used to predict subsequent performance, achievement tests are used to evaluate an individual's status following completion of learning or training (e.g., after completion of a school course or company training program). This difference is reflected by the different types of validation procedures used: Predictive criterion-related validity is most frequently used to validate ability tests, while content validity is more commonly used with achievement tests. (As will be seen below, however, achievement tests are sometimes used for prognostic purposes).

Finally, a previously frequently-held misconception regarding the differences between achievement and ability tests was that achievement tests measure the effects of learning while ability and aptitude tests measure innate capabilities which are independent of learning. However, recent thought is that all tests which assess current behavior include elements of previous learning. Thus, ability and aptitude tests cannot be considered as merely measures of innate abilities, but rather as measures of a combination of abilities resulting from both heredity and previous learning.

Uses of Achievement Tests

Achievement tests are used for a variety of reasons; however, these reasons typically involve educational or training situations:

1. First, achievement tests are used to provide information on academic accomplishment. In this context, achievement tests help an instructor assess how much a student knows about a particular subject or how well he or she can perform a particular task. Achievement tests

are frequently used to aid instructors in assigning student grades.

Also related to this use of achievement tests are the concepts of summative and formative evaluation. Testing is done at the end of a unit or course of study to determine if students have attained instructional goals which represents summative evaluation. In contrast, if testing is done several times during the instruction in order to help the instructors determine what learning is still needed to reach these objectives; this type of testing is referred to as formative evaluation. Traditionally, testing in educational settings has been summative rather than formative.

2. Achievement tests also are used to assess the effectiveness of instructors and instructional programs. Related to this use, achievement tests help instructors adapt instructional programs to fit the needs of the student (e.g., provide remedial instruction).

3. Finally, the use of achievement tests can actually facilitate learning by providing students with feedback regarding their overall strengths and weaknesses. Studies have shown that feedback is useful in increasing formal learning and student motivation.

Types and Examples of Achievement Tests

There are four major types of achievement test (Aiken, 1982):

1. **Survey Test Batteries**: Survey test batteries consist of several subject-matter achievement tests designed to be administered to particular grade levels. The goal of survey test batteries is to assess an individual's standing relative to a particular group. Examples:

    Iowa Tests of Basic Skills: The Iowa Tests evaluate five types of basic skills considered important to most academic performance – vocabulary, reading comprehension, language skills, work-study skills, and mathematics skills. These tests are used in grades 3-8. **California Achievement Tests**: This test covers reading, arithmetic and language and was developed for use with students in Grade 1 through college sophomore level. The California Achievement Tests were designed to assess educational attainment and to diagnose difficulties in basic skill areas.

2. **Single Survey Tests**: Single survey achievement tests evaluate students on individual subjects. These tests are usually longer and more detailed than same-subject tests included in survey test batteries; thus, single survey tests permit a more complete evaluation of a student's achievement in a particular subject area. Single subject tests typically yield one score. Examples:

   Course Final Exams

   Professional Licenser and Certification Tests

   College Entrance Examination Board Achievement Test: The CEEB consists of one-hour achievement tests in 15 areas (e.g., Literature, American History, French).

3. **Diagnostic Tests**: Diagnostic tests used to identify specific student strengths and weaknesses in a particular subject area. Thus, diagnostic tests usually provide several scores, one for each subskill or skill component assessed by the test. Generally, administration of a diagnostic test follows administration of a survey test battery: After determining that a student's achievement in a particular subject area is lower than expected or desired, a diagnostic test would be administered to better evaluate the deficiency. Examples:

Diagnostic Reading Scale: This diagnostic test provides four major scores (word recognition, oral reading, silent reading and auditory comprehension) and two supplementary scores (rate of silent reading and phonics).

Metropolitan Instructional Test: This test provides items in three skill areas – reading, math, and language.

4. **Prognostic Tests**: Prognostic tests are used to predict achievement in specific areas; as predictors, they are most like aptitude tests. However, in terms of content (academic-oriented), such tests are most similar to other achievement tests. Examples:

Modern Language Aptitude Test: This test was designed to assess the potential of an English-speaking student for learning a foreign language.

Readiness Tests: Readiness measures (e.g., reading-readiness) help assess whether a student possesses the skills needed to succeed in a particular educational program or task.

Measures of Ability and Aptitude

Although the terms "ability" and "aptitude" are frequently used interchangeably, ability tests generally measure the ability or "power to perform a task," while aptitude tests measure the ability or "power to learn to perform a task" (Brown, 1970). Thus, ability tests assess the individual's current state and aptitude tests predict the individual's future state based upon his or her current state. However, both ability and aptitude tests, in contrast to achievement tests, measure the results of a combination of two factors – the individual's inherited capabilities and his or her previous general learning experiences. Ability and aptitude tests include measures of general intelligence as well as measures of general and specific abilities.

Construction of ability and aptitude tests relies on a "trait and factor view" of abilities and aptitudes. In other words, any particular aptitude is composed of a variety of interrelated skills, abilities and characteristics which are relatively stable over time. In fact, it is this assumption of stability which led to the previously discussed misconception that aptitudes and abilities are inherited characteristics which do not change over time. However, although abilities and aptitudes no doubt do have genetic-related components, they are also the result of learning experiences and the interactions between the innate capabilities and environmental situations and experiences. Thus, the stability of abilities and aptitudes must not be merely assumed to be due to their inherited nature, but rather as a reflection of the fact that people tend to lead generally consistent lives. Indeed, studies have shown that aptitudes can be altered by changing environmental conditions (e.g., Anastasi, 1958; Bloom, 1964).

Intelligence Testing

1. Definition of Intelligence:

Discussions of intelligence frequently avoid providing a definition of this term. This is no doubt due to the fact that, like many other psychological terms, intelligence has yet to be assigned a single, unanimously agreed upon meaning. Thus, intelligence has been viewed in a variety of ways: e.g., reasoning ability, and, most commonly (although perhaps least precise), "general mental ability."

Some theories have suggested that the concept of intelligence exists only within the framework provided by intelligence tests – i.e., intelligence is what intelligence tests measure. However, even within this narrow definition (in which intelligence is equated with an IQ score), the meaning of intelligence is imprecise. For example, an IQ score of 120 obtained on one intelligence test is not necessarily equivalent to an IQ score of 120 on another test, intelligence is equated with "IQ" and these terms will be used interchangeably.

2. **Stability of Intelligence**:

In contrast, however, shifts in IQ have been frequently noted. In their longitudinal "California Guidance Study," Honzik, MacFarlane and Allen (1948), for example, found that 59% of 222 subjects showed change in IQ scores of at least 15 points between ages 6 and 18. Research examining such fluctuations in IQ has indicated that the greatest changes are most often related to two factors: changes in health and changes in environmental conditions.

Age Decrements: An important issue related to intelligence and intelligence testing is the relationship between mental abilities and chronological age. Many early *cross-sectional* studies suggested that intelligence tends to increase only until middle or late adolescence and thereafter gradually decreases (e.g., Jones and Conrad, 1933; Wechsler, 1958). In contract, *longitudinal* studies have indicated that decreases in intelligence typically do not occur until after age 60 (e.g., Bayley and Oden, 1955), or even until the period just preceding death.

Finally, studies evaluating the existence of age decrements in intelligence after age 60 have suggested that declines in mental abilities are more associated with health factors than to chronological age itself (Schaie and Gribbon, 1975).

In addition to the important educational and cultural issues raised by population declines in test scores (such as the one discussed above), two implications relevant to IQ (and other mental ability testing are suggested: 1) Mental ability test norms require periodic updating, and 2) experiential variables must be considered when interpreting an individual's test scores (Anatasi, 1982).

3. **Variables Related to Intelligence**:

Sex: Typically, differences between males and females on tests of general intelligence are insignificant. However, in terms of specific cognitive and perceptual-motor abilities, females tend to be superior in verbal fluency, reading comprehension, finger dexterity, and clerical skills, while males tend to be superior in mathematical reasoning, visual-spatial ability, and speed and coordination of large motor movements (e.g., Minton and Schneider, 1980). It should be noted that these differences are, at least in part, the result of differences in cultural influences and opportunities.

Birth Order: Several researchers (e.g., Altus, 1966) have found that, in general, first-born children are brighter that later-born children. Parental differences in child-rearing practices (e.g., greater attention paid to first-borns) are considered a major contributor to this observed difference in intelligence.

Socioeconomic Status: One of the most consistent findings of research related to intelligence and group differences is a positive correlation between IQ scores and socioeconomic level. Whether this correlation is due primarily to genetic or environmental factors is yet to be determined; however, it is generally agreed that higher level socioeconomic status is associated with more favorable home environments which have significant positive effects on general mental health.

Race: One of the most controversial issues related to intelligence and group differences is the relationship between IQ and race (especially Black Americans). Based on a summary of pre-1960 literature related to black-white differences, Dryer and Miller (1960) concluded that whites tend to be superior to blacks in psycho-physical, psychomotor and intellectual abilities. Subsequently, researchers have interpreted such findings either in terms of hereditary or environmental influences.

A strong supporter of the genetic position is A. R. Jensen (1969) who has concluded (based in large part on data collected by Sir Cyril Burt (1966) that the frequency of genes carrying higher intelligence is generally lower among blacks than whites. Jensen's controversial conclusions have been widely criticized. Arguments against Jensen stem primarily from two issues: 1) the validity of the data on which he based his conclusions (e.g., the irregularities in Burt's data; the adequacy of standard IQ tests to measure the intelligence of individuals with varying levels of test-taking motivation and skill), and 2) Jensen's failure to fully consider the influence of environmental factors on intelligence (e.g., maternal dietary deficiencies) (Needlemam, 1973).

4. **Other Issues Related to Intelligence Testing**:

Culture-Fair Tests: An important consequence of the issue of race and intelligence has been a recent increased concern with the validity of standard IQ tests to assess the intelligence of individuals who come from other than white, middle-class backgrounds. As a result of this growing concern, numerous attempts have been made to design "culture-fair" (originally referred to as "culture-free") tests which contain only items related to experience common to a wide variety of cultures.

A number of culture-fair tests utilize a nonverbal format as an attempt to overcome cultural-loading associated with the use of language (e.g., Raven Progressive Matrices). However, some research has suggested that nonverbal tests are often actually more culturally-loaded than verbal tests (e.g., Miller, 1973, Berry, 1972). It has been found, for example, that black children (as well as children from low Socio-economic status backgrounds) generally find the performance subtests of the WISC (nonverbal tests) as difficult as the verbal subtests.

Due to a wide variety of often subtle factors which influence test performance (e.g., cultural differences in test-taking motivation and interest, problem-solving approaches), attempts to develop truly culture-fair tests have been unsuccessful.

PL 94-142: In 1975 the 94th Congress passed the Education for All Handicapped Children Act (PL 94-142). Among other things, the Act provides that 1) an Individual Educational Plan (IEP) be provided for each handicapped student in the public education system; 2) that the IEP should provide education for the student in "the least restrictive environment"; and 3) that, although use of psychological tests for assessment is acceptable, no assignment to special classes can be made on the basis of a single IQ test alone. Although PL 94-142 is aimed primarily at handicapped children, the law clearly specifies that any test used must also be valid, reliable and non discriminatory with regard to non-English speaking and minority group children.

5. The Stanford-Binet History:

The 1905 Binet-Simon Scale: In 1904, Alfred Binet was appointed by the French minister of public education to a commission formed to recommend procedures for identifying retarded children so they could receive special education. In collaboration with T. Simon, another appointee, Simon developed the Binet-Simon Scale, relying primarily on two principles which today still serve as guidelines for the development of ability and intelligence tests: 1) the principle of *general ability* (the Binet-Simon Scale included items which measured ability on a variety of tasks; performance on each item correlated not only with performance on other items, but also with the combined results or total score); and 2) the principle of *age differentiation* (i.e., older children have greater capabilities than younger ones; the test thus included a set of tasks that could be completed by an increasingly higher proportion of children as age increased). The 1905 scale consisted on 30 tasks arranged in ascending order of difficulty. Although some sensory and perceptual tasks were included, the majority of the items were verbal in nature.

The 1908 Revision: In 1908, the number of tasks (tests) were increased and all tests were grouped in terms of age level rather than in order of increasing difficulty. The criteria for including a test at each age level was that the test was successfully passed by approximately 75% of a representative group of children at that age level. As a result of this age scale, a child's score could be expressed in terms of a *mental age* (MA) which was determined by comparing an individual's performance with the average performance of normal individuals at specific age levels. (Calculation of a MA score involves first determining the individual's *basal age* or the highest age or year level at which the individual successfully passes all tests. The test then continues until the individual successfully passes all tests. The test then continues until a *ceiling age* is reached; i.e., the year level at which all tests are failed. MA is then calculated by adding to the basal age the designated amount of "credit" earned for each test passed between the basal and ceiling ages).

The 1977 Revision: Only minor changes were made at this time, including the addition of new tests at certain age levels, and the extension of the scale to the adult level.

Terman's 1916 Stanford-Binet Intelligence Scale: The most widely accepted English version of the Binet-Simon Scale is L.M. Terman's 1916 revision which retained many of the primary features of the Binet-Simon – the principles of general mental ability and age differentiation, and the use of "mental age." The most important addition in 1916 was the inclusion of the concept of *intelligence quotient* ("IQ") which used an individual's mental age in conjunction with his or her chronological age (CA) to obtain a ratio score which was believed to reflect his or her rate of mental development relative to other individuals of the same age. The *ratio IQ* is computed as follows: IQ = MA/CA x 100. Thus, if a child's chronological age is 8, his Stanford-Binet mental age is 4, his IQ = 50. Because the 1916 revision had a maximum MA of 19.5, anyone over this age would have an IQ less than 100. In response to this problem, and because it was believed at the time that mental age ceased to improve after age 16, 16 was used as the maximum chronological age when computing the IQ.

The 1937 Scale: Although the 1937 revision was subsequently revised in 1960 and re-standardized in 1972, the test's current form and psychometric adequacy (reliability and validity) can be directly traced to this revision. Important changes made in 1937 included: 1) an extension of the age range downward to age 2 (increased "floor") and increased MA upward to age 22 years, 10 months (increased "ceiling"), as the result of an addition of tasks to the test; 2) an addition of performance items to help decrease the test's emphasis on verbal ability although it continued to primarily reflect verbal ability; 3) improvement of scoring standards and instructions to improve standards of administration sample, however, representatives of the sample were still limited in terms of SES (higher than general American SES), race (native-born whites only), and residence (excess of urban dwellers); and 5) provision of two comparable forms (L and M) to determine the test's reliability and standard error of measurement.

The 1960 Revision: 1960 revisions included: 1) combination of the best tests from Forms L and M into single L-M Form; 2) further improvements in scoring and administration instructions; 3) extension of the IQ tables from age 16 to age 18; and, perhaps most importantly, 4) introduction of the concept of *deviation IQ* which was already used in the Wechsler scales to correct the problems associated with the ratio IQ (i.e., improve comparability between age levels due to differences in standard deviations at different age levels, and elimination of the problems associated with the MA ceiling).

The deviation IQ: The Stanford-Binet deviation IQ is a standard score with a mean of 100 and standard deviation of 16. New IQ tables (Pinneau Revised IQ Tables) were constructed so that differences in variability at different age levels were corrected and IQ scores could be compared across the various age levels. (Note: Due to the error of measurement of a Stanford-Binet IQ, a 10-point band should be allowed on each side of an obtained IQ score. For example, the "true" score for an obtained IQ of 100 would be expected to fall between 90 and 110.)

1972 Revised Norms: New norms were established based on a sample of approximately 2,100 subjects who were more representative of the United States than earlier normative samples. The 1972 sample was stratified in terms of community size, geographic region, economic status and race (the sample included Blacks, Mexican-Americans and Puerto Ricans). An IQ score derived for any particular individual using the 1972 norms tends to be lower than if earlier norms are used because, in general, the 1972 norm subjects had higher test scores than earlier norm subjects (especially preschool-aged subjects). The authors attribute this to, among other factors, the influence of the mass media, and increased literacy and educational backgrounds of parents. The deviation IQ mean remained at 100 and the standard deviation at 16, however.

Administration and Scoring: Each year or age level contains several tests (including an alternate test). To pass a test, the examinee must pass a certain minimum number of tasks (e.g., to pass test 1 of year 11, the examinee must pass at least 1 of the 2 tasks which made up test 1).

Administration first involves determination of the examinee's basal age; i.e., the highest year level at which he or she successfully passes all tests. To decrease administration time and reduce examinee fatigue and boredom caused by beginning the test at too low an age level, the examiner must be skilled at determining the appropriate year level at which to begin the test. After the basal age has been established, the examiner presents higher age level tests until a level is reached at which all tests are failed – this is the ceiling age, at which point testing is stopped.

The 1960 revision includes year Levels II through XIV, with an Average Adult Level, and three levels of Superior Adult. Levels II through V are further broken down into half-year intervals. Year levels II through XIV contain six tests each, the adult levels contain between 6 and 8 tests. The test is scored as it is administered. A specific amount of MA credit is allowed for each test passed beyond the basal age.

Psychometric Properties: The psychometric properties of the Stanford-Binet were assessed following the 1937 revision. In general, the scale proved to be a highly reliable instrument with an average alternate forms (Forms L and M) reliability coefficient of .91. However, reliability was found to be more stable for older age groups and for individuals with lower range IQ scores (less than 70). Because of its high reliability for lower IQ individuals, perhaps, the Stanford-Binet is widely used in educational classifications of the mentally retarded. The Stanford-Binet is still considered to be one of the most reliable psychological instruments of any kind.

Validity of the Stanford-Binet has been established in several ways: In addition to content and construct validity and factor analytic support of validity, the Stanford-Binet has been shown to have concurrent and predictive validity. Studies correlating Stanford-Binet IQ scores with school grades, teacher's ratings and achievement test scores have generally yielded correlation's coefficients of .40 to .75, with highest correlation's between IQ and performance in verbal-type academic courses (e.g., English, history, literature).

6. **The WAIS and WAIS-R**:

History: The original Wechsler-Bellevue Intelligence Scale was developed by David Wechsler at Bellevue Hospital in

New York in 1939. The test was designed to evaluate the intellectual abilities of older children and adults (16-75) and to serve as an alternative to the Stanford-Binet which had been shown to be unsuitable for evaluating the intellectual ability of normal and superior adults. The Wechsler-Bellevue introduced the concept of *deviation IQ* which permits an assessment of an individual's intellectual standing relative to not only his or her peers but also to other age groups.

The Wechsler-Bellevue was replaced by the Wechsler Adult Intelligence Scale (WAIS) in 1955. The WAIS corrected many of the deficiencies of the original test and replaced items which were difficult to score or interpret. In addition, the newer test utilized a larger standardization sample which covered a wider geographical area and included non-white subjects.

Within five years of its introduction, the WAIS had become one of the most frequently used psychological tests. It is currently one of the most widely used tests in not only educational, but also mental health settings.

Test Description: Similar to Binet, Wechsler viewed intelligence as the ability to act purposefully and to adapt to the environment. Wechsler also believed that general intelligence consists of several interrelated functions or elements; by measuring an individual's ability on each of these functions, his or her intelligence could be assessed. Thus, the WAIS and WAIS-R consist of 6 verbal subtests and 5 nonverbal or performance subtests, each of which is believed to represent one of the important functions of general intelligence. Figure 1 below lists the subtests and the major function (s) each subtest assesses (Kaplan and Saccuzzo, 1982):

Figure 1

SUBTEST	FUNCTION
Verbal Scale:	
INFORMATION	Range of general knowledge and "common sense"
COMPREHENSION	Judgment (application of past experience to present situation)
ARITHMETIC	Concentration, problem-solving skills, arithmetic ability
SIMILARITIES	Abstract and logical thinking
DIGIT SPAN	Attention span, immediate memory, anxiety
VOCABULARY	General intelligence, vocabulary level
Performance Scale:	
DIGITAL SYMBOL	Visual-motor functioning, ability to learn new task
PICTURE COMPLETION	Perceptual discrimination
PICTURE ARRANGEMENT	Visual perception, planning ability
BLOCK DESIGN	Nonverbal reasoning (ability to analyze and organize)
OBJECT ASSEMBLY	Visual analysis and coordination (analysis of part-whole relationships), persistence

Administration and Scoring: While administration of the WAIS involved presentation of all verbal subtests first and then all performance subtests, administration of the WAIS-R alternates verbal and performance subtests. The primary purpose of this change in administration was to enhance examinee interest. On all tests, except Digit Span and Object Assembly, items are presented in order of difficulty.

Each subtest includes a different number of items and has its own scoring instructions (e.g., some subtests permit "time bonuses" for quick performance). To allow comparability between subtests, raw scores are converted to standard or *scaled scores* (mean = 100, standard deviation = 3) using a conversion table. Thus, at any age level, a scaled score of 10 is equivalent to the 50th percentile for all subtests. Scale scores are summed and converted into three IQ scores – Verbal IQ, Performance IQ, and a combined Full Scale IQ.

Wechsler believed intelligence test performance declined with age and IQs are therefore computed based on a declining age standard; i.e., IQs are computed separately for 10 different age groups in order not to "penalize" older examinees. Deviation IQ scores were derived from a norm sample which had a mean of 100 and standard deviation of 15.

Interpretation:

Individual Subtests: Wechsler subtests are assumed to measure specific intellectual skills and an analysis of performance on subtests can provide information on a subject's particular strengths and weaknesses. Examples of possible clinical interpretations for each subtest are provided below:

Information: This test taps old learning and performance.

It reflects one's cultural and educational background. Although memory is involved to some extent, scores are not greatly affected by age unless the subject is psychotic or a victim of degenerative brain disorder. High scores can be viewed as evidence of intellectual ambition.

Comprehension: Poor performance on this subtest might indicate long-term dysfunctions such as early brain injury or childhood psychosis, or might indicate a poor or alternated cultural background. Psychotics generally score low on this subtest due to its requirement for judgmental decisions. Pathological conditions might be suggested by bizarre responses.

Arithmetic: A low arithmetic score might indicate mental retardation, brain injury or organic disorder, or less severe disturbance such as concentration problems or a transitory anxiety state.

Similarities: The capacity to think abstractly, which is required by this subtest, might be affected by long-term deterioration, severe brain dysfunction or emotional disorders.

Digits Span: This subtest is extremely sensitive to anxiety and brain deterioration. Performance on Digits Forward and Digits Backward is also affected by left hemisphere brain damage while decreased performance on Digits Backward only, might indicate localized right hemisphere injuries. Good Digit Span scores relative to other subtest scores in a schizophrenic subject is also associated with absence of anxiety.

Vocabulary: Vocabulary is considered one of the most stable aspects of intelligence and this subtest is thus one of the last tests to be affected by emotional disturbances or brain damage. Low Vocabulary scores are associated with poor general intelligence, poor education, a non-English speaking culture and/or early brain injury. High Vocabulary scores indicate high verbal intelligence and a good educational background. Thought disturbances are revealed by such behavior as bizarre expressions, perseverations, and concreteness of thinking.

Digit Symbol: Digit Symbol is the most sensitive subtest to dominant hand motor problems. Low scores might be associated with conditions ranging from anxiety to brain damage.

Picture Completion: This test is the subtest least sensitive to focal brain disorders; it is, however, sensitive to paranoia and schizophrenia.

Block Design: Block Design performance is affected by organic impairment, especially for subjects with diffuse or parietal lobe injuries; for most brain injuries, Block Design will be the performance subtest on which the lowest score is achieved.

Picture Arrangement: Picture Arrangement is often considered a measure of "social intelligence." Poor performance might indicate certain left hemisphere injuries which disrupt social skills.

Object Assembly: Organic and schizophrenic patients generally score low on this subtest; some research has indicated that neurotics and depressed individuals also do poorly.

Verbal IQ vs. Performance IQ: Discrepancies between

Verbal and Performance Scale scores might be indicative of cultural and educational deficiencies, emotional problems or brain damage. For example, if an individual scores low on the Verbal Scale (e.g., less than 70), an immediate interpretation might be that the examinee is mentally retarded. However, if his or her Performance Scale score is in the normal range, educational, language or cultural deficits (not mental retardation) might be responsible for the low Verbal score.

In addition, a Verbal IQ higher than Performance IQ is associated with right hemisphere impairment or diffuse brain damage, while a Verbal IQ lower than Performance IQ is associated with left hemisphere impairment (Guertin, et al., 1966, 1971). Brain damage is most often indicated by lower Verbal, higher Performance IQ. This latter pattern has also been associated with juvenile delinquency (Gorotto, 1961) and sociopathy (Kahn, 1968).

(It should be noted that the WAIS is not considered to be sufficiently accurate to diagnose organicity and is, thus, best used as a screening instrument for deficits in an individual known to be brain-damaged.)

Pattern Analysis: Wechsler believed that pattern analysis of subtest scores could be used to assess and diagnose certain emotional problems. For example, schizophrenia is associated with impaired judgment and concentration and, therefore, schizophrenics would be expected to perform poorly on the Comprehension and Arithmetic subtests. Research, however, has generally not supported Wechsler's proposed patterns. In spite of this lack of empirical evidence, many clinicians continue to interpret WAIS subtest score patterns.

Psychometric Properties of the WAIS and WAIS-R:

Norms: The WAIS standardization sample included 1700 individuals distributed of 7 age levels (ages 16-64). The sample characteristics approximated the 1950 census in terms of educational and occupational levels, geographic region, urban-rural ratio, and race. The sample included an equal number of males and females and each age level included two institutionalized mentally retarded examinees. Supplemental norms were established for an "old age" sample of 475 subjects, aged 60 and over.

The standardization sample for the 1981 revision of the WAIS, the WAIS-R, was based on the 1970 census and consisted of a representative sample of 1880 individuals distributed of 9 age groups (16 years 0 months, through 74 years, 11 months).

Comparison of the WAIS and WAIS-R:

Classification of Intelligence: Changes in intelligence classifications were made for evaluating WAIS-R Full Scale IQs. These changes are marked with an asterisk in Figure 2 below.

Figure 2

IQ	WAIS	WAIS-R
130 and above	Very Superior	Very Superior
120-129	Superior	Superior
110-119	Bright Normal	*High Average
90-109	Average	Average
80-89	Dull Normal	*Low Average
70-79	Borderline	Borderline
69 and below	Mental Defective	*Mentally Retarded

With the order of administration of the two scales counterbalanced, the obtained IQs were:

Figure 3

	WAIS IQs	WAIS-R IQs
Verbal Scale	108.7 + 14.0	101.8 + 15.0
Performance Scale	113.4 + 14.2	105.4 + 16.5
Full Scale	111.0 + 14.1	103.8 + 16.4

These figures indicate that WAIS IQs are about 7-8 points higher than WAIS-R IQs. However, more research is needed before these results can be considered.

Advantages and Disadvantages of the WAIS:

Advantages of the WAIS over other measures of intelligence include the following:

- The WAIS offers an IQ which is the standard against which the majority of other IQ tests are measured;
- The WAIS yields more than merely a full-scale IQ: it provides subtest scores and Performance and Verbal Scale IQs which can provide diagnostic information.
- The WAIS is both the most comprehensively normed adult intelligence test available today and one of the most extensively researched intelligence tests available.

Disadvantages of the WAIS include the following:

- The test is suitable only for individual administration and is extremely time-consuming.
- The test is heavily influenced by cultural and language

concepts which are unfamiliar to many minority group individuals.

- The WAIS appears susceptible to improvement in performance with retesting; since alternate forms are unavailable, use of the WAIS in reevaluation situations is difficult.
- The WAIS has been found to overestimate low IQs and caution should be taken when interpreting scores of adults who test below an IQ of 80. The test also tends to underestimate IQs at upper levels.
- Validity coefficients have generally not been particularly impressive.

7. Comparison of the WAIS and Stanford-Binet:

- Both tests have proven to be highly reliable.
- The Stanford-Binet is more verbal in content than the WAIS.
- Because the WAIS (and WAIS-R) utilize a point scale (rather than an age scale which is used by the Stanford-Binet), these tests provide scores on individual functions of intelligence (i.e., subtest scores). The WAIS also provides Verbal and Performance Scale scores in addition to a Full Scale score; the Stanford-Binet provides only one total score.
- Older subjects tend to score higher on the WAIS than the Stanford-Binet while the reverse is true for younger subjects. This may be attributed to a) the declining age standard used in the WAIS, and b) the standardization samples used (the Stanford-Binet Sample consisted of younger subjects).
- Brighter individuals tend to obtain higher IQs on the Stanford-Binet while duller ones do better on the WAIS.

- With an unselected adolescent or adult population, the correlation between WAIS and Stanford-Binet scores is approximately .80. The Stanford-Binet correlates highest with the WAIS Verbal Scale, lower with the Performance Scale.

8. **The WISC, WISC-R and WPPSI**:

WISC: The Wechsler Intelligence Scale for Children was designed for use with children aged 5 to 15 years, 11 months. The test includes ten subtests plus two supplemental tests.

Figure 4

Verbal Scale	Performance Scale
Information	Picture Completion
Comprehension	Picture Arrangement
Similarities	Block Design
Vocabulary	Object Assembly
Arithmetic	Coding (or)
Digit Span (optional)	Mazes

WISC-R: The WISC was revised in 1974; the major changes included the following: 1) age range changed to 6 years through 16 years, 11 months 30 days, providing some overlap with the WAIS-R; 2) 38% new items written to replace obsolete and unclear items, eliminate items that seemed to be differentially unfair to different groups of examinees, and include female and black figures in pictures used in certain of the subtests; 3) length of several subtests increased to improve reliability; and 4) re standardization between the WISC-R and the WISC range from approximately .80 to .90;

between the WISC-R and the Stanford-Binet between .60 and .78. However, the range of IQs appears to be greater on the Stanford-Binet than the WISC-R, with brighter children obtaining higher IQs on the Stanford-Binet and duller children obtaining higher IQs on the WISC-R.

The WISC-R takes approximately one hour to administer; Verbal and Performance Scale subtests are administered in alternating order.

WPPSI: The Wechsler Preschool and Primary Scale of Intelligence was first published in 1937. This scale was designed to assess the intelligence of children aged 4 through 6 ½ years; i.e., when the child is beginning formal schooling and accurate measures are needed for educational decisions. The format and subtests of the WPPSI are similar to the WAIS and WISC except that 1) the Digit Span Test has been replaced by a sentences subtest, and 2) the Performance Scale consists of five subtests, only the first three of which are included in the WOSC (Picture Completion, Block Design, Mazes, Animal House and Geometric Design). With regard to administration, testing takes approximately 50 to 75 minutes, and Verbal and Performance subtests are altered.

B. **Other Tests of Ability**

1. **Infant and Preschool Tests**: Most tests designed for use with infants and children of preschool age assess a wide variety of motor, social and cognitive skills. Problems associated with testing young children are typically caused by short attention span, susceptibility to fatigue and low test-taking motivation. Perhaps for these reasons, infant tests tend to be associated with low reliability and validity

coefficients. As discussed earlier, infant test scores are not generally considered to be valid predictors of later intellectual ability.

Brazelton Neonatal Assessment Scale: The BNAS was developed as an intelligence test for infants aged 3 days to 4 weeks old. In addition to its use as an intelligence assessment tool, the BNAS is frequently used in both medical and psychological research. The BNAS contains 47 items related to the infant's neurological, social and behavioral functions (e.g., reflexes, startle reactions, hand-motor coordination, cuddliness). Like most other infant ability tests, the Brazelton has limited evidence of predictive and construct validity and reliability.

Gesell Developmental Scales: The Gessel Developmental Scales provide a standardized method for observation and evaluation of children, aged 4 weeks through 6 years. Information on the child's motor, adaptive, language and personal-social related behaviors is obtained through direct observation of the child's responses to a variety of stimulus objects and from data obtained from the child's mother. This scale appears to be most useful in the identification of neurological and other organically-related behavioral deficits.

Bayley Scale of Infant Development: The Bayley Scales are used to assess the developmental status children aged 2 months to 2 ½ years. Three separate scales are provided: 1) the Mental Scale which assesses perception, memory, language, problem solving, verbal communication, and abstract thinking; 2) the Motor Scales which measures gross motor abilities and manipulator skills of the hands and fingers, and 3) the Infant Behavioral Record, a rating scale completed by the examiner which assesses various aspects of the child's personality development. These Scales are particularly helpful in assessing current sensory and neurological deficits, emotional disturbances, and environmental deficits.

McCarthy Scales of Children's Abilities: The MSCA, for children aged 2 ½ to 8 ½, consists of 18 tests, grouped into six overlapping scales (verbal, quantitative, perceptual-performance, general cognitive, memory and motor). The General-Cognitive Scale is most similar to other measures of general intellectual development and scores on this scale are reported in terms of a General Cognitive Index (GCI).

Cattell Infant Intelligence Scale: This scale, designed as a downward extension of the Stanford-Binet, is for infants from 2 to 30 months old. Scores are reported in terms of MA and IQ. The test is considered to be a screening device.

Vineland Social Maturity Scale: The Vineland, designed at the Training School in Vineland, New Jersey, is used as a means of assessing and guiding the development of normal and handicapped children and adults, particularly in terms of their ability to look after personal needs and participate in activities which lead to independence as an adult ("social competence"). Although the Vineland was originally designed to aid in the assessment of feeblemindedness and in differentiating between mentally deficient individuals who are and are not socially adequate, the Scale is currently used with both normal and mentally deficient populations (birth to age 25). Clinical used of the scale has indicated that the test is particularly useful for younger-aged individuals and with the mentally retarded.

Items included in the Vineland represent eight categories

which represent factors contributing to social maturation and adjustment to the environment – general self help, self-help in eating, self-help in dressing, self-direction, occupation, communication, locomotion, and socialization. Items are arranged in order of normal life progression. Information needed to score each item is obtained from an informant familiar with the child (parent, caretaker, etc.). The score obtained is expressed as a social age (SA) which can be converted to a social quotient (SQ), using a formula similar to a ratio IQ (SA/CA x 100 = SQ).

A primary disadvantage of the Vineland is that naiveté or bias on the part of the informant can affect ratings. However, such deficiencies can be minimized by extensive clinical training of the examiner.

Relationship between the Vineland and Stanford-Binet: Correlations between the Vineland and the Stanford-Binet vary widely, but are generally sufficiently low to indicate that different facets of behavior are being measured by the two instruments. Used in conjunction with the Stanford-Binet, the Vineland has proved helpful in diagnosing mental retardation and in making decisions regarding institutionalization. For example, an individual who scores as mentally deficient on the Stanford-Binet might receive a Vineland Scale age score which indicates that he or she could adjust satisfactorily outside an institution.

Denver Developmental Screening Test: The DDST is a screening device designed to detect developmental delays during infancy and childhood (birth through 6.4 years). Using the DDST, a child is evaluated as "normal", "questionable" or "abnormal", based on his or her performance on items in four behavioral areas – personal-social, fine motor-adaptive, language, and gross motor. The Denver test has been used in

Head Start programs, well baby clinics, community health centers, and by pediatricians, medical students, and other health workers. Items are scored by direct observation of the child. A "developmental delay" is scored if the child fails an item which 90% of children normally pass at a younger age. Assignment of a "questionable" or "abnormal" score is made based on the presence of delay scores.

The test constructors believe that a primary advantage of the DDST is that it can be administered by nonprofessional health aides who have received only a few hours of training.

Tests for the Handicapped:

A number of tests have been developed as alternatives to the Stanford-Binet, Wechsler and other major scales for testing individuals with mental and physical handicaps.

Columbia Mental Maturity Scales (CMMS): This pictorial classification test was originally developed for use with cerebral-palsied children, aged 3 through 12. It is also useful for assessing the abilities of children with speech and language impairments and hearing loss. The test consists of 92 cards containing three, four or five drawings. The examinee is required to identify the drawing which does not "belong with" the other items. A distinguishing feature of the Columbia scale is that it does not require either verbal responses or fine motor skills. The purpose of the test is to assess general reasoning ability. Scores are expressed in terms of Age Deviation Scores (mean = 100, standard deviation = 16).

Peabody Picture Vocabulary Test: Similar to the Columbia scale, the PPVT is a multiple-choice test which requires the examinee to indicate the correct answer in some manner. This test, developed for use with severely handicapped individuals aged 2 ½ to 18 years, contains 150 plates, each containing four pictures. The examiner provides a stimulus word and the examinee responds by pointing to the correct picture. (Because of its reliance on verbal instructions, the PPVT is not suitable for the hearing impaired.) Raw scores can be converted to mental age scores, deviation IQs or percentiles. Studies examining the relationship between the PPVT and the Stanford-Binet and Wechsler have indicated a wide variety of correlation coefficients, ranging from .22 to .92. The PPVT has been used in a number of research situations with normal, mentally retarded, emotionally disturbed and physically handicapped subjects.

Haptic Intelligence Scale for Adult Blind: This nonverbal intelligence test was designed to be used in conjunction with the Verbal Scale of the WAIS. The Haptic Scale involves a tactile approach to testing and includes six performance tests (Digit Symbol, Block Design, Object Assembly, Object Completion, Pattern Board, and Bead Arithmetic).

Hiskey-Nebraska Test of Learning Aptitude: The Hinskey-Nebraska was designed as an intelligence test for use with deaf and hard-of-hearing children aged 3 to 16. The test includes twelve subtests: Bead patterns, Memory for Color, Picture Identification, Picture Associations, Paper Foldings, Visual Attention Span, Block Patterns, Completion of Drawings, Memory for Digits, Puzzle Blocks, Picture Analogies, and Spatial Reasoning. Items chosen for inclusion in the subtests were selected primarily on the basis of age discrimination.

Use of the Stanford-Binet and Wechsler Scales for the Blind: Both the Stanford-Binet and Wechsler Scales have been adapted for use with the visually impaired. The Hayes-Binet test contains items from forms L and M which can be administered without the use of vision; the test includes six tests for each level from VIII through XIV and eight tests for the Average Adult Level. The Majority of the tests are oral, although a few use Braille materials. The Wechsler adaptations consist primarily of items drawn from the Verbal Scale. Other tests of ability which have been adapted for use with the visually impaired include the SAT, SCAT, and GRE.

Nonverbal and Culture-Fair Tests:

In the past several decades, there has been increased concern about the adequacy of standard tests for assessing the ability of individuals from subculture, minority or disadvantaged backgrounds. Traditionally, tests developed to overcome the problems associated with testing such individuals have focused on the language, speed and content of tests (Anastasi, 1982). This focus has been based on the assumption that cultures not only differ in terms of language and literacy, but also in terms of values placed on rapid performance and familiarity with objects typically included in ability test questions. Thus, developers of culture-fair tests have often focused on these three factors to eliminate biases associated with ability testing.

Leiter International Performance Scale: This scale was developed through several years of use with Hawaiian ethnic groups, African and other national groups. The distinctive feature of the Leiter is non-reliance on either verbal instructions or responses. All subtests of the Scale involve the use of a response frame and all tests are administered by having the examinee attach appropriate response cards to the frame. Tasks include matching colors, picture completion, number estimation, spatial relations, and memory for series. In addition to its cross-cultural uses, because of the nonverbal nature of the test, the Leiter is also useful for testing the deaf and language disabled. The Scale was designed for use with individuals aged 2 through 18 years; scores are reported in terms of Mental Age scores and ratio IQs. The *Arthur Adaptation* of this Scale is suitable for use with children aged 3 through 8 years. Criterion-related validity coefficients are reported to range from .52 to .92.

IPAT Culture Fair Intelligence Test: This paper and pencil test, developed by R.B. Cattell, includes three scales for three age levels: Scale I (ages 4 to 8 and mentally retarded), Scale II (ages 8 to 13 and average adults), and Scale III (ages 10 to 16 and superior adults). Scale I includes four subtests considered as "culture fair" by Cattell. Scales II and III each contain a ratio IQ; Scales I and II provided deviation IQ scores. The tests are highly speeded and extensive instructions are required. The Culture Fair Intelligence Test has been successfully used in several European countries, certain African and Asian countries, Australia and America. However, American Black children from lower socioeconomic levels tend to score no higher on this test than on the Stanford-Binet.

Progressive Matrices: Progressive matrices were developed as a measure of Spearnman's "g" factor of intelligence. The test includes 60 matrices, each missing a section. The examinee chooses the missing portion from the alternatives provided. Less difficult matrices require accuracy of discrimination; more difficult matrices involve analogies, permutations and other logical relationships.

Norms are provided for individuals' ages 8 to 65 years.

Goodenough Draw-A-Man Test: This test requires the examinee to "make a picture of a man; make the very best picture that you can." Scoring is based primarily upon the child's accuracy of observation and conceptual thinking. Seventy-three scorable items were chosen on the basis of their ability to differentiate between ages. A revised scale, the Goodenough-Harris Drawing Test, also requires the examinee to draw a woman and him/herself. Research has suggested the Draw-A-Man test correlates highest with tests of reasoning, spatial aptitude, and perceptual accuracy. Unfortunately, studies examining the "culture-fairness" of the Goodenough-Harris test have shown that cultural and socioeconomic level biases are not entirely overcome by this test.

Black Intelligence Test of Cultural Homogeneity: The BITCH was designed as a culture-fair intelligence test for Blacks. In its development, black and white examinees were compared in terms of their understanding of slang used by Black Americans. The test contains 100 words which were originally selected from the Dictionary of Afro-American Slang. The BITCH can be considered a "culture specific" test on which black examinees outperform white examinees. One of the goals of this test is to identify children who have been unfairly placed in classes for the mentally retarded on the basis of standard IQ test scores.

System of Multicultural Pluralistic Assessment: SOMPA's developer, sociologist Jane Mercer (1979), was particularly concerned with the misclassification of children from minority and other sub-cultural backgrounds as mentally retarded solely on the basis of IQ test scores; an underlying assumption of this instrument is that all individuals, regardless of cultural background, have the same average potential and that observed differences in ability are the result of cultural and social experiences.

SOMPA was designed for use with children aged 5 through 11. The test relies on both parental interview and individual evaluation of the child. Perhaps the most unique feature of the SOMPA is its integration of three models of assessment – medical, social, and pluralistic. The **medical model** component of the SOMPA is concerned with the perceptual-motor development and health conditions which might affect the child's learning abilities. Thus, the test includes a health history, visual, hearing and motor tests. The **social system** component of the SOMPA is concerned with the child's social adaptive behaviors. The WISC-R (or WPPSI) is used to assess the child's adaptive behavior in terms of his or her school-related role; the Adaptive Behavior Inventory for Children is also used to obtain additional information. Finally, the **pluralistic** component is concerned with the child's socio-cultural background. An Estimated Learning Potential (ELP) is derived, based on a comparison of the child's obtained WISC-R score and the score predicted for the child based on scores of children from similar socio-cultural and ethnic backgrounds.

Group Ability Tests Used in the School Kindergarten Through Grade 12:

Kuhlmann-Anderson: This multi-level test battery was designed as a group intelligence test for use with 8 levels – kindergarten through grade 12. KAT items are generally more nonverbal than items contained in similar tests and thus require minimal language and reading skills. Scores are expressed in terms of verbal, quantitative and total scores; at some levels the total score can be converted to deviation IQs or percentile bands. The KAT has been found to correlate highly with other tests, especially the Stanford-Binet.

Henmon-Nelson Test: The H-NT contains four levels (K-2, 3-6, 6-9, and 9-12). It produces a single score considered to reflect general intelligence. Raw scores can be converted to deviation IQs and percentiles.

College Level Tests:

College Board Scholastic Aptitude Tests: The SAT is one of the most researched group ability tests. The purpose of the test is to predict potential for higher education for high school seniors; as a predictor, the test is considered an aptitude test. The SAT provides two scores – a Verbal score (based on items covering sentence completion, identification of opposites, analogies, and paragraph comprehension) and a Mathematical score. Research has shown the SAT to be very stable instrument with reliability coefficients ranging from the high .80's to low .90'sw. Validity of the SAT for predicting freshman college grades is increased when SAT scores are combined with high school grades. A primary criticism of the SAT revolves around its relatively poor discrimination of college grades for students who score in the middle range.

Graduate Record Examination: The primary purpose of the GRE is to assess general scholastic ability. It is probably the most widely used test for graduate school entrance; normally, GRE scores are considered in conjunction with grades, letters of recommendation and other academic factors. In addition to the general test, the GRE offers advanced tests in approximately 20 subject areas. In spite of its extensive use, the predictive validity of the GRE has not been consistently shown to be high (Kaplan and Saccuzzo, 1982).

Miller Analogies Test: Although the Miller Analogies Test is primarily used for the selection of college graduate students, the test has also been used for selection and evaluation of high-level industry personnel. The Miller Analogies Test consists of complex analogies items derived from a variety of academic areas. Percentile norms are provided for graduate and professional school students in several fields and for industrial employees/applicants.

School and College Ability Tests: The SCAT is a group intelligence test for grades 9 through 12. It yields three scores: verbal, quantitative and a total score. The quantitative score is derived from a quantitative comparison test which evaluates the student's fundamental number operations abilities. The verbal score is derived from a verbal analogies test. Like most other intelligence tests, the SCAT primarily reflects the student's educational experiences. The SCAT is available in large-type and Braille editions for use with the visually handicapped.

Group Ability Tests Used in Industry and Career Counseling:

Otis Self-Administered Test of Mental Ability: This test has been used primarily in personnel screening for a variety of jobs including clerk, assembly-line worker and foreman. Validity studies have indicated that while the test may be effective for semi-skilled jobs in predicting ability to learn a job and ease of initial adaptation, the test does not appear to be related to subsequent job achievement. The best known adaptation of the Otis is the Wonderlic Personnel Test, a 12-minute test of mental ability for adults. The Wonderlic has been widely used in industry to aid employee-related decisions.

General Aptitude Test Battery: The GATB consists of eight paper-and-pencil tests and four apparatus tests. The 12 tests provide scores on the following nine factors: intelligence, verbal aptitude, numerical aptitude, spatial aptitude, form perception, clerical perception, motor coordination, finger dexterity, and manual dexterity. Raw scores are converted to standard scores which can be compared to scores associated with 36 occupational ability patterns. These patterns were derived from an evaluation of GATB scores of individuals employed in over 8000 different types of jobs. The test was designed for use with high school seniors and adults and is useful for vocational counseling and placement.

Flanagan Tests: The Flanagan Aptitude Classification Test (FACT) consists of 16 tests which correspond to job elements determined to be critical to job performance (e.g., inspection, coding, memory, assembly). The Flanagan Industrial Tests (FIT) were derived from FACT; although the FIT tests measure the same job elements as the FACT, they take less time to administer and tend to be more difficult.

"We are none of us all of a piece; more than one
person dwells within us, often in uneasy
companionship with his fellows."
Somerset Maugham

Section 2
Personality and Clinical Measures

Measures of Personality:

Anastasi (1982) defines personality tests as "instruments for the measurement of emotional, motivational, interpersonal and attitudinal characteristics."

History: The use of personality tests can be traced back to WWI when the Woodworth Personal Data Sheet was developed in response to a need for an instrument to identify emotionally unstable recruits. Items included in this early instrument were chosen on the basis of a "logical-content strategy" in which items were interpreted in terms of their face validity only. This technique test construction quickly fell into disfavor, however, and current personality tests are generally developed on the basis of more sophisticated techniques including empirical criterion keying, factor analysis, content validation, and application of personality theory.

Issues Related to Personality Tests: The development and use of personality tests is associated with a variety of problems. First, in comparison to ability testing, personality is far more susceptible to "faking." Also, the behavior assessed by personality tests is often quite changeable over time. Thus, random or temporary changes in behavior at the time of testing might be misconstrued as permanent personality factors. An additional problem is related to the fact that the non-cognitive factors tapped by personality tests are far more "situation specific" than the cognitive factors assessed by ability tests (Anastasi, 1982). Finally, numerous ethical issues have been raised by the use of personality tests. For example, personality testing has been criticized in educational and industrial settings where such tests are used to make student/employee decisions in spite of the fact that validity of the tests in such situations have not been shown.

Personality tests are generally one of two major types: self-report inventories or projective techniques.

Self-Report Inventories:

Minnesota Multiphasic Personality Inventory: The MMPI was developed by Hathaway and McKinley at the University of Minnesota Hospitals in the late 1930s and early 1940s and was first published in 1943. The test is composed of 550 true-false self-report items. The primary purpose of the MMPI is to aid the clinicians in distinguishing between normal and non-normal individuals. More specifically, the MMPI was designed to facilitate diagnosis of the major psychiatric/psychological disorders.

As an example of a structured personality inventory, the MMPI contrasts with projective techniques (e.g., Rorschach) which utilize ambiguous stimuli and relatively unstructured formats and which are subject to flexible interpretations depending on the theoretical orientation of the clinician. While both projective and objective, structured tests have as a primary goal the understanding and prediction of human behavior, objective tests tend to be better suited for diagnosis and classification because they provide far more accurate and quantifiable data than projective tests.

Test Description: Originally, MMPI items were listed on cards and examinees were asked to sort the cards into three categories – "true", "false" and "cannot say". Later a booklet form was developed to permit group administration. A tape-recorded version is also currently available which allows examinees to listen to questions. The test was designed for individuals aged 16 and over who have at least a 6th grade education.

MMPI items consist of descriptive statements covering a wide range of content areas (e.g., health, psychosomatic symptoms, motor disturbances, political and social attitudes) and are generally worded as follows; "I frequently find myself worrying about something", "I am happy most of the time", "I do not tire easily", "I believe I am being plotted against."

In its regular administration, the MMPI provides scores on 13 scales – 10 clinically and 3 validity. The 13 scales and their interpretations when an elevated score is obtained are described in Figure 5 (Kaplan and Saccuzzo, 1982).

A major innovation of the MMPI was its inclusion of validity scales to identify certain test-taking attitudes. The Lie Scale (L) consists of 15 items which make an examinee appear in a favorable light. High scorers on the L Scale (many "False" responses) are presenting themselves in an excessively "pure" manner (e.g., never lie, get angry, feel like swearing). The F scale consists of 64 items which are all rarely responded to in the scorable direction. High F scores may result from extreme eccentricity, idiosyncrasy, psychiatric illness, response carelessness or scoring errors. The original purpose of the F Scale was to assess response conformity. Scores on the L and F Scales which exceed a specified value invalidate other scale scores. Finally, the K Scale consists of 30 items designed to assess the examinee's need to either present him or herself in a favorable light (high K) or to attest to many personal defects or weaknesses (low K). K scores are used to compute a correction factor which is added to certain clinical scale scores to obtain adjusted scores. In addition, if a large number of items are not answered or are responded to with a "cannot say", the test may be considered invalid.

Figure 5

Scale	Interpretation
Clinical Scales:	
1 Hypochondrias is	Physical Complaints
2 Depression	Depression
3 Hysteria	Immaturity
4 Psychopathic Deviate	Authority Conflict
5 Masculinity-Femininity	Masculine or Feminine Interests
6 Paranoia	Suspicion, hostility
7 Psychasthenia	Anxiety
8 Schizophrenia	Alienation, withdrawal
9 Hypomania	Elated mood, high energy
0 Social introversion	Introversion, shyness
Validity Scales:	
L Lie Scale	Tendency to present self in favorable light
F False Scale	Response carelessness
K K Scale	Defensiveness

Scoring and Interpretation: After raw scores have been determined, a profile is constructed based on converted T or standard scores (man = 100, standard deviation = 10). Generally, a T score of 70 or higher is considered indicative of a pathological deviation. However, the clinical significance of a score actually differs from scale to scale; e.g., a score of 75 on Scale 8 (Schizophrenia) is not necessarily indicative of an extreme abnormality.

Maximum use of the MMPI is made by analyzing patterns of scores rather than individual scores. To facilitate interpretation of score patterns, numerous systems of profile coding have been developed. The primary distinction between systems is the complexity of symbolization used. Generally, coding systems involve listing scales in descending order of magnitude of scores. A simple coding system uses only the two highest scale scores to form the code (e.g., a profile with the highest score on Scale 6 and the second highest score on Scale 1 would be classified as "61"). The primary advantage of coding is that it provides an objective classification of MMPI profiles and enables clinicians to identify behavior patterns which typify a particular profile code which, in turn, provides a basis for interpreting test scores.

The Atlas for Clinical Use of the MMPI (Hathaway and Meehl, 1951) represents an early approach to interpretation using coded profiles. A clinician uses the Atlas by referring to profiles which are similar to that of the examinee. Similar codebooks, many based on more systematically collected data than the Atlas, have been developed, some for specific populations (e.g., college students, high school students).

Several computerized systems are also available for MMPI interpretation. These systems vary. Some, for example, provide information to be used primarily for screening purposes and offer only brief descriptive summaries. Recognizing the possible dangers of computerized analyses, The APA has set out guidelines for computer - based test interpretation services (APA, 1966).

Test Development and Norms: Hathaway and McKinley collected a large number of self-reference statements from various sources. From the original pool of items, 504 items were selected based on their non ambiguity and independence from one another. Two groups of subjects were identified: The "clinical" group was composed of patients who had been diagnosed as belonging to the following clinical categories – hypochondria, depression, hysteria, psychopathic deviation, paranoia, psychasthenia, schizophrenia, and hypomania. The "normal" group consisted of relatives and visitors of patients, WPA workers, high school graduates attending pre-college conferences, and medical patients. The 504 item questionnaire was administered to both groups and item analyses were conducted to identify items that discriminated between the clinical and normal groups, and between one particular diagnostic group and the other diagnostic groups. This procedure is known as empirical criterion keying; i.e., the selection of test items on the basis of their ability to discriminate between criterion group subjects and normal subjects. In subsequent years, additional items were added to the original 504 items.

Reliability and Validity: Studies evaluating the reliability of the MMPI have generally not been promising, especially in terms of long-range reliability. Graham (1977) found that typical test-retest reliability coefficients for intervals of one day to two weeks ranged from .70 to .85; however, longer intervals (one year and over) yielded coefficients of only .35 to .45. In terms of internal consistency, Dahlstrom, et al. (1977) reported a wide range (-.5 to .96) with typical coefficient values ranging from .60 to .90.

The primary source of validity comes from numerous research studies which have focused on the construct validity of the MMPI. In fact, it is evidence from these studies which has maintained the reputation of the MMPI in spite of its otherwise poor psychometric performance.

Advantages and Disadvantages of the MMPI: The MMPI is perhaps the most widely used self-report personality inventory. Its primary advantages include: 1) it can be used for a variety of purposes – e.g., research, diagnosis, screening and counseling; 2) the MMPI has demonstrated that personality can be assessed by an objective, empirically-based procedure; 3) the MMPI contains validity scales which reflect distortion; and 4) the test has provided a pool of items which have been used in the development of other scales.

The major criticisms of the MMPI include: 1) Test-retest reliability studies have indicated low coefficients which should caution the clinician concerning the reliability of the scales; 2) standard scores were derived from a normative sample which may not be representative of other populations in terms of age, sex, educational background, socioeconomic status or ethnicity; 3) high intercorrelations among certain clinical scales decrease their effectiveness in differential diagnosis; and 4) interpretation of MMPI scores requires a high level of psychological sophistication and care must be taken (especially in case of automated profiles) that MMPI scores are not misused by untrained users.

California Psychological Inventory: The CPI was designed for use with normal individuals aged 13 to adult. Approximately one-half of the 480 true/false items were drawn from the MMPI items. The CPI's 18 scales include three validity scales and 15 personality scales (e.g.,

Dominance, Sociability, Responsibility, Socialization, Self-Control). CPI scores are reported in terms of standard scores. The test has been successfully used to predict delinquency, parole outcome, academic grades, and probability of high school dropout.

Edwards Personal Preference Schedule: In contrast to the MMPI which was developed on the basis of empirical criterion keying, the EPPS is an example of a personality test which was developed on the basis of personality theory. Items included in the EPPS represent 15 needs drawn from the manifest need system originally proposed by Murray and his associates at the Harvard Psychological Clinic (e.g., need for Achievement, Exhibitionism, Autonomy, Affiliation, Nurturance). The test includes 210 pairs of statements in which items representing each of the 15 needs are paired with items representing the other 14 needs. The examinee chooses the statement which best describes him or herself. Need scores are interpreted in terms of percentile or T-score norms for college men and women. The EPPS uses a forced-choice format designed to control the effects of an examinee's tendency to respond in a socially desirable way.

Personality Research Form: The 20 personality variables included in the PRF were derived from extensive research of personality theory. Twelve of these variables are the same traits included in the EPPS. The PRF manual provides descriptions of high scorers for each trait plus a set of defining trait adjectives. T-Scores were derived from a sample of approximately 1,000 male and 1,000 female college students.

Rorschach: Hermann Rorschach, a Swiss psychiatrist, experimented with inkblots which he administered to different psychiatric groups between 1911 and 1922. Although Rorschach never developed a specific theory concerning the test, he thought that the way an individual interprets the inkblots reveals something about his or her behavior and/or mental state. Rorschach believed the test introduced a new technique for psychiatric diagnosis and the study of perception in general and, for this reason, he administered the test to both patients and non patients.

Since the 1921 publication of Rorschach's book, Psycho diagnostic, many books and thousands of articles have been written on the Rorschach test. The Rorschach remains the most commonly used psychological test available to clinicians. Sundberg (1961) surveyed 185 clinical facilities and found that 93% of them used the Rorschach. Ten years later, Lubin, et al. (1971) surveyed 251 clinical facilities and found that 90% were using the test.

Test Description, Administration and Scoring: The Rorschach tests consist of 10 cards, each containing a bilaterally symmetrical inkblot printed on a white background. Five of the inkblots are black and gray only, two contain areas of bright red, and three combine several pastel shades.

The test is administered individually in two stages: during the first stage, the free-association phase, the examiner presents cards in a prescribed order and the examinee is asked to describe what he or she sees. The examiner keeps a verbatim record of the examinee's responses, spontaneous remarks, emotional expression, and other behaviors. During the second stage of administration, the inquiry phase, the examiner scores the examinee's responses. While the examiner is required to limit communication during the first phase, during the inquiry phase the examiner actively questions the examinee in order to obtain information needed for scoring.

There are numerous approaches to scoring the Rorschach. Most often examinees are scored in terms of at least five factors or dimensions:

Location: Where in the inkblot the examinee's perception is located. In scoring location, the examiner determines if the examinee used the whole blot (scored as a W), a common detail (D), an unusual detail (Dd), or if the examinee's perception was over generalized from the whole ("confabulatory response") (DW).

Determinants: What in the inkblot determined the examinee's response? Four properties, the inkblot's shape, movement, color and shading, may determine a response. If an examinee uses only one aspect of the inkblot to make a response, a score of F (pure Form) is assigned. Movement is scored as either human movement (M), animal movement (FM) or inanimate (m). The scoring category of determinants is probably the most important because it assesses the perceptual-cognitive process that the examinee employs to select and classify stimuli.

Form Quality: How similar a perception is to the actual shape of the inkblot. Scores of F+, F or F- are assigned, depending on the extent of the match between the response and inkblot.

Content: The category the perception falls into – human (H), animal (A), or nature (N).

Frequency of Occurrence: The extent to which the perception was original or "popular" (i.e., frequently seen in normative samples).

Interpretation: Interpretation of the Rorschach is a complex task. Following a review of all test data, interpretation generally involves two phases: 1) The prepositional phase in which the clinician attempts to develop hypotheses about the examinee from the results of the test and the manner in which the examinee responded, and 2) the integration phase during which all hypotheses are integrated into a global description of the subject.

Interpretation is a highly individualized matter dependent on the focus of the clinician. Some clinicians rely on actuarial patterns and signs while others depend primarily on intuition. In addition, clinicians may emphasize, for example pattern scores, individual responses, or content. Obviously, it is during interpretation that the Rorschach drops on objectivity. Exner, author of <u>The Rorschach: A Comprehensive System</u> (1974), advocates both a quantitative analysis, which has a high reliability, and a qualitative analysis, in which the theoretical orientation of the clinician can produce greater variability of interpretation.

Psychometric Properties: Goldfried, et. al. (1971) have presented a survey of available data on norms, reliability and validity for a variety of applications of the Rorschach. These authors conclude that several Rorschach indices have demonstrated sufficient validity to justify their use for research purposes; however, their effectiveness in clinical use has not been sufficiently established. Buros (1970) has similarly concluded that the "vast amount of writing and research has produced astonishingly little, if any, agreement among psychologists regarding the specific validates of the Rorschach."

Validity of the Rorschach test has been difficult to establish for a variety of reasons. First, there are numerous statistical problems associated with scoring which render validity data questionable. Secondly, direct validity evidence is often not feasible since criterion measures reflecting unconscious motivating factors measured by the test are unavailable. Thirdly, because interpretation of the Rorschach is highly individualized, validity studies generally do not evaluate the Rorschach test, but also evaluate a particular examiner's interpretation of the test. Finally, changes in the testing situation can affect an examinee's responses and therefore affect the test's effectiveness in measuring basic personality structures (Masling, 1960).

Holtzman Inkblot Test: Various modifications have been made of the Rorschach test involving such factors as permitting group administration and providing more objective scoring. A major modification is the Holtzman Inkblot Test (Holtzman, 1959) which differs from the original Rorschach in the following ways: 1) 45 cards, rather than 10, are used (two parallel series available); 2) the examinee is allowed only one response per card; 3) scoring is limited to a few number of dimensions (location, form appropriateness, from definiteness, color, shading, and movement energy level); and 4) quantitative scoring weights are used. In spite of efforts to increase the psychometric properties of the Holtzman (in comparison to the Rorschach), studies have suggested that it may not be more valid than the Rorschach (e.g., Gamble, 1972).

Thematic Apperception Test: The TAT was introduced by

Christina Morgan and Henry Murray in their 1935 article, "A Method for Investigating Fantasies: The Thematic Apperception Test." The TAT is based on Murray's theory of needs and has two primary goals 1) the understanding of the examinee, and 2) the prediction of the examinee's behavior based on that understanding. The TAT has proven to be particularly useful in the prediction of hostility and achievement.

Test Description and Administration: In comparison to the Rorschach test, the TAT is Murray's third version of the test (1943) which consists of 20 cards, 19 of which contain vague black and white pictures and one blank card. Normally the test is administered in two one-hour sessions, with ten cards being presented at each session. The cards presented in the second session are generally more evocative and bizarre than the cards presented in the first session. Four sets of cards are available – boys, girls, males over age 14, females over age 14.

Instructions given to the examinee are non directive so as to evoke an unhindered response from the examinee. Murray proposed that "normal" adolescents and adults be told that the test is a "test of imagination" while psychotics and adolescents and adults with subnormal intelligence be told that the test is a "story-telling test." The examiner can ask direct questions if he or she believes that such inquiry will facilitate production of responses. The examiner either writes the stories as the examinee shares them and presents the various pictures. In group administration, examinees record their own stories. Group administration has been used to assess group processes and characteristics; in this type of administration, the group tells a story following presentation of pictures involving groups.

Scoring and Interpretation: There are even more scoring systems for TAT than for the Rorschach. Generally, however, scoring and interpretation begins with identification of the "hero: of the examinee's story. Next, the content of the responses are interpreted in terms of Murray's "needs" (e.g., achievement, affiliation) and "press" (environmental forces which influence the satisfaction of needs). In analyzing the importance of a given need or press for an examinee, attention is focused on 1) the intensity, duration and frequency of its presence in the examinee's stories, and 2) the uniqueness of its presence in certain stories. It is generally assumed that unusual responses have greater interpretive significance. In general, the majority of scoring and interpretation methods rely primarily on the thematic content of the stories.

A number of quantifiable scoring systems have been developed. In McClelland's system (1953), for example, the examinee's story is assigned one point for "achievement imagery" and ten additional points if the following variables are present: need for achievement, successful or unsuccessful anticipatory goal state, instrumental activity with various outcomes, obstacles or blocks, nurturant press, affective states and achievement theme. Since most quantifiable scoring methods are quite time consuming and complex, they are generally unpopular with clinicians. Thus, interpretation of the TAT most often depends on the examiner's theoretical orientation, obviously not a very objective criterion.

Psychometric Properties: Determination of TAT validity has been a difficult task for a variety of reasons: First, it is difficult to determine whether an examinee's stories represent manifestations of his/her personality or whether they are merely stereotypic responses to the scenes depicted on the cards. Second, even if the stories do represent an examinee's personality, is it appropriate to assume that the examinee identifies with his or her "hero" or that the needs and press expressed actually represent the examinee's situation? Third, like other projective techniques, the TAT is sensitive to temporary emotional and motivational conditions which affect TAT responses; thus, results obtained might not reflect the examinee's enduring personality traits. Finally, since the purpose of the test is to provide a general description of the examinee's personality, the problem of an appropriate criterion becomes crucial. As a result of these issues and others, most psychometric evaluations of the TAT have provided inclusive and conflicting results.

The TAT has been extensively used in personality research related to the assumptions which underlie TAT interpretations (e.g., identification with the story hero). While such studies have contributed to the construct validation of the TAT, the construct validity of the TAT seems questionable in light of other research which has found little correlation between the TAT and the EPPS and Adjective Check List (e.g., Megargee and Parker, 1968).

Clinical Measures:

Halstead-Reitan: Halstead believed that humans have a "biological intelligence" which is not adequately measured by simple IQ tests and which is directly related to the integrity of the functioning of the brain. Thus, tests included in the Halstead-Reitan battery are those which were effective in differentiating between brain-damaged and control subjects. For each test on which an examinee scores above a specified cutoff point, a value of .1 is assigned. The summation score for all tests provides an "Impairment Index." Separate batteries are available for adults, children aged 9 through 14 and children aged 5 through 8. Tests included in the battery are: category test, tactile performance test, Seashore rhythm test, speech sounds perception test, finger oscillation test, trial making test, and strength of grip test. The Halstead-Reitan Battery is normally used in conjunction with an IQ test (e.g., WAIS) and various sensory-perceptual tests such as the Sensory Imperception Procedure or the Tactile Finger Recognition Test.

Luria-Nebraska: The Luria-Nebraska battery consists of 269 items which were selected on the basis of their importance in diagnosis. Each item represents an important aspect of the following 11 skill areas: Motor functions, rhythm, tactile functions, visual functions, receptive speech, expressive speech, writing, reading, arithmetic, memory, and intellectual processes. Raw scores for each item can be converted to scaled scores from 0 to 2, with a score of 0 suggesting that the examinee is functioning within the normal range and a score of 2 suggesting brain injury. Scores are also summed for the 11 skills areas plus three other summation scores (right-hemisphere, left-hemisphere and pathognomic scores); the 14 summed scores are plotted on a profile graph which permits comparison to T score. In comparison to the Halstead-Reitan, the Luria-Nebraska 1) takes less time to administer (2 ½ hours instead of 6 hours), 2) is more highly standardized in terms of content, administration and scoring, and 3) provides more complete coverage of neurological deficits and more precise identification of brain damage (Anastasi, 1982).

Illinois Test of Psycholinguitic Abilities: Based on C.E. Osgood's three-dimensional model of psycho linguistics, the ITPA contains several subtests: auditory association, verbal expression, grammatic closure, auditory reception, visual reception, visual sequential memory, auditory sequential memory, visual association, visual closure, manual expression, auditory closure, and sound blending. This diagnostic test is particularly useful for children aged 2-10 with learning disabilities. The ITPA was specifically designed to assess psycho linguistic abilities and inabilities of moderate and mildly handicapped children. Scores are reported in terms of standard scores, age scores and psycho linguistic age scores.

Boston Visual Retention Test: This test is used to evaluate spatial perception, immediate recall, and visual-motor skills. The Benton includes ten cards, each containing one or more simple geometric figures which the examinee is requested to reproduce after 10 seconds exposure. Performance is evaluated in terms of number of cards correctly reproduced and total number of errors. Scores falling a given number of points below the expected level for the examinee are considered significant; however, corroborative evidence from other sources is required for an exact diagnosis.

Bender Visual Motor Gestalt Test: The Bender-Gestalt was originally designed as a measure of visual-perceptual skills based on Gestalt theory. It currently enjoys a much wider range of uses including diagnosis of brain damage, psychiatric disorders, mental retardation and malingering, assessment of intelligence and school readiness. The Bender-Gestalt is used as both an objective and projective test: As an objective test, it is used to detect brain dysfunction and to estimate intelligence. As a projective technique, the Bender-Gestalt is used as a nonverbal measure of personality.

The test consists of nine geometric figures which the examinee is asked to reproduce. Numerical scoring methods have been developed; one of the most popular is based on drawing errors which were found to distinguish between normal and abnormal subjects (Pascal and Suttell, 1951). Developmental norms are available which define the number of errors expected to be produced by children aged 5 to 8; up to age 8, a few errors generally considered "normal", after age 8, errors suggest an abnormality (e.g., a mental age less than 8, organically, emotionally disturbance).

The Bender-Gestalt, like the Benton test, has been shown to be an effective screening device for the detection of brain damage. (Studies evaluating the use of these two tests with adult psychiatric patients have reported a median "hit rate" of 75 (Heaton, Baade and Johnson, 1978). The Bender-Gestalt is particularly useful when used as part of a test battery or in conjunction with other tests such as the MMPI or measures of organic brain dysfunction.

Measures of Interest

An important issue in educational and career counseling is the measurement of interests. To assess interests, numerous interest inventories have been developed. The two most popular inventories were actually developed quite early – The Strong Vocational Interest Blank (SVIB) was first introduced in 1927 and the Kuder Preference Survey in 1939.

Strong-Campbell Interest Inventory:

The Strong-Campbell Interest Inventory (SCII) is a revision of the Strong Vocational Interest Blank (SVIB); it was developed primarily to overcome some of the shortcomings associated with the SVIB. Changes made in the revised SCII include 1) merging of items from the men and women's forms into a single instrument to reduce sex biases; and 2) incorporation of Holland's theory of vocational choice to provide the test with a theoretical basis.

The SCII consists of 325 items grouped into 7 parts. In the first five parts, the examinee selects his or her preferences with regard to occupation, school subjects, activities, amusements and types of people by marking each statement as "like", "dislike" or "indifferent". In the remaining two parts, the examinee expresses his or her preferences for paired activities and responds to self-descriptions (e.g., win friends easily, have patience teaching others). All scores are expressed as standard scores. SCII scores are reported in terms of six General Occupational Themes which correspond to Holland's six personality factors (realistic, investigative, artistic, social, enterprising, and conventional), 23 Basic Interest Scales, and an Occupational Profile. The Occupational Profile indicates the amount of similarity between the examinee's responses and those of individuals actually employed in the occupations. (Scores on the six General Occupational Themes and 23 Basic Interest Scales compare the examinee's scores with those of people in general).

Kuder Occupational Interest Survey (KOIS):

The KOIS is a modification of the original Kuder Preference Record. While the Kuder Preference Record provided an index of an examinee's general interest in terms of ten general interest areas (outdoor, mechanical, scientific, etc.) the KOIS more closely resembles the SCII in that it also provides an index of the similarity between the examinee's interests and the interests of individuals employed in a variety of occupations. In addition, the KOIS provides a separate set of scales for college majors so that the test may also be used to guide examinees in their selection of a college major. The KOIS uses a forced-choice format, requesting examinees to select one of three activities as their most preferred and one as their least preferred. The test contains 100 triads.

Although research on the KOIS is not as extensive as that on the SCII, studies have suggested that this test is an effective tool for high school and college career counseling.

Word Association Tests

Word Association Test: A projective test of emotional reactions in which the subject responds to a stimulus word with the first word that comes to mind; sometimes called a free association test.

The most common procedure is to set up a free association situation with the subject seated comfortably or reclining, sometimes in a darkened room. The examiner reads from a prepared list and records the subject's replies, the time taken to respond to each word ("latency of reply"), and any speech or behavior mannerisms he observes. Some examiners also repeat the test shortly after it is completed, instructing the subject to respond with same words previously given. The object is to see whether responses to certain key words are changed.

The word association test was invented by Francis Galton in 1879 as a means of exploring individual differences. Emil Draepelin was apparently the first to apply it to the study of abnormality, in 1892. When psychoanalysis came into prominence, Carl Jung began to use the technique as a clinical tool. His original list of one hundred words was designed to uncover complexes by presenting emotion-provoking words scattered among neutral words. See JUNG.

The most widely used form of the test is the one devised by Kent and Rosanoff in 1910. Their list consists of one hundred neutral, familiar nouns and adjectives (table, fruit, cold, eagle, tie) which, unlike Jung's list, are not selected to tap possible areas of conflict. These words were presented to a group of a thousand normal subjects, and a frequency tally for each word was made – for example, "needle" led to 160 responses of "thread", and 158 of "pin", but only one each of blood, broken, camel, and weapon. On the basis of such investigations, tables of common and uncommon responses have been constructed.

In scoring the Kent-Rosanoff Free Association Test, the table is used to determine the number of "individual reactions" (zero frequency), and the median frequency value for the total set of responses. Special tables have also been constructed for children and normal people of different age and races. Other scores are computed for failure to react, doubtful reactions, nonspecific reactions (general words such as "good" or "useful" given to every stimulus word). When the test is used for detection of complexes, some of the indications cited by Jung may be applied: long reaction time, very short reaction time, repetition of stimulus word before responding, extremely personal responses, clang responses, behavioral signs of excitement or embarrassment, whispered or shouted responses, stammering, laughing, inability to recall the response on the post-test. Hull and Lugoff (1921) showed that these measures correlate fairly highly with each other and are important clues to the unconscious dynamics of the subject. Once a complex is isolated, the therapist explores the sensitive area through interviews.

The word association technique is sometimes administered, along with other procedures, in diagnosing mental illness. Rapaport, Gill and Schafer (1946) have devised a special list of sixty words for this purpose. It includes a number of familial, anal, oral, aggressive, and sexual terms. According to Schafer, there is some indication that obsessive-compulsive patients give ostentatious reaction such as dance-terpsichore, house-domicile, and often have delayed responses when several possibilities come to mind at once; hysteric patients are apt to hesitate over words with sexual connotations and often give infantile reactions or use evaluative words such as snake-slimy, or cockroach-hate. Common reactions among schizophrenic patients are: blocking, highly unique responses, clang associations (bite-light), phrase completions (taxidermist), personal association (masturbations-loss). (In the latter example the subject was disturbed by the loss of semen). On other applications of the test, schizophrenics were found to give twenty-five to thirty individual reactions, while normal adults with elementary school education gave 5.2 and the college educated 9.3 individual reactions.

A number of variations on the method have been tried. Thurstone (1952) used words that could be interpreted in different ways – a technique called "homographic free association" – to tap social attitudes; for example, "revolution" could evoke either "social upheaval" or "turning around". Goodenugh (1942, 1946) developed a similar test for masculinity-femininity; for example, the response to "bow" could be either "hair ribbon" or "arrow". Others have used lists of words that sound alike (homophones), such as "sell" and "cell"; Foley and MacMilian (1943) found that on this form of the test many people gave responses in line with their vocational interests. A forced-option, multiple-choice technique has been applied to testing such dimensions as masculinity-femininity and normality-abnormality, but this variant is of doubtful value since it limits freedom of expression.

The Word Association technique has been used for other purposes than personality study and psycho diagnosis. As early as 1907 Munsterberg applied it to guilt detection. The usual method here is to scatter "giveaway" words among neutral words and to compare the reaction time of the subject to each of these types. However, studies by Marston (1938) and others have shown that the technique is not conclusive, since there is no regular relation between guilt and reaction time, and sophisticated subjects can often control their responses. The test is therefore highly questionable when used alone, but has some value when applied in conjunction with physiological measurements.

In addition, the test is sometimes used in market research to discover reactions to company names or brand names; in social psychology as a means of uncovering prejudices or other social attitudes; and in police investigations as a means of identifying drug addicts, homosexuals, and criminals, since these individuals tend to respond to stimulus words with their own special style.

Choice of Stimuli

Although any set of words is, in theory, appropriate for use as word association test (WAT) stimuli, in fact, experimenters often refer to a standard set of words, so as to be able to make use of normative data available for those words. For example, extensive information is available for the 100 stimulus words of the Kent-Rosanoff list (Palmo & Jenkins, 1964; Russell & Jenkins, 1954). Since these words are predominantly nouns and adjectives, Palermo and Jenkins (1964) have constructed a new list of stimuli of other grammatical classes and have gathered extensive normative data on these words. Bousfield, Cohen, Whitmarsh, and Kincaid (1961) also have compiled a frequently used stimulus.

In clinical studies, the Menniger word list (Rapaport, Gill, & Schafer, 1946) has been a common source for stimulus words. Again, the availability of normative information as well as the classification of the stimuli into certain affective categories has enhanced the usefulness of this list.

Although these lists provide the most widely used sources for stimuli, there are a variety of other stimulus-word lists with normative information available. These have been listed toward the end of the references, under the heading "Normative Data". In addition, a number of experimenters will select idiosyncratic stimuli which are especially suited to the needs of their particular investigations.

Format of Association Test

Association tests may be divided into two general classes - free association and controlled association. In *free* association, the subject is free to give a response from any semantic or grammatical category. It is left unspecified as to what kind of response should be given. In *controlled* association, the subject is limited as to the type of response which is acceptable. The limitation may be in terms of instructions to choose a response from a particular category (e.g., antonyms), or it may be in terms of presenting a test in which the response alternatives are specified (e.g., as in a multiple-choice test).

Free Association

Within the free – association method, there are several

different procedures employed. Probably the more frequently used procedure is that in which the subject is given a single stimulus word and asked to respond as rapidly as possible with the first single word which comes to mind. This procedure is an example of a *discrete* free-association test (any single-word response is acceptable). Other types of free-association tests are used, however, and the resulting picture of the associative domain has been found to differ according to the format of the test. For example, in *continued* association, the subject is presented with the same stimulus word a number of times and must continue to give associative responses to the original stimulus. Sometimes he is instructed not to give the same responses; sometimes no instructions are given. The number of responses elicited may be determined by the number of times the stimulus is presented or by the interval of time allowed for the subject to make responses. In the method of *continuous association*, the stimulus term is presented only once; the subject uses this word as a point of departure for a chain of associative responses, only the first of which may be directly determined by the nominal stimulus. As before, the number of responses is determined, in part, by the length of the response interval allowed.

Discrete Association: A well-known study where the method of discrete free association was used is that of Russell and Jenkins (1954), in which the single responses of 1,008 subjects were used to establish the Minnesota norms to each stimuli of Kent-Rosanoff WAT. Subsequent normative studies (e.g., Palermo & Jenkins, 1964, in preparation) have also utilized this method.

Continued Association: The method of continued association is well exemplified in the work of Noble (e.g., 1952), in which the mean number of responses elicited by a stimulus during a 60-second interval was taken as an index of the "meaningfulness", m, of that stimulus. These m values have been found to be remarkably stable over time and consistent from one investigation to the next.

As a variant on this method of continued association to measure meaningfulness, Archer (1960) and Noble (1961) have asked subjects to rate stimuli in terms of their associative power. In Archer's study, association value, a, is based on the number of subjects who indicate the stimulus evokes at least one response; in Noble's study, the rated association value, $m1$, is based on how many associations the stimulus evokes in the mind of the subject. The agreement between m, $m1$, and a is high; Noble (1963) notes correlations of .90+ between m and $m1$, the correlation between m and a is smaller, due to the fact that a is a very insensitive measure at the upper end of the associative scale. S.S. Shapiro (1964), using nonsense and real word CVC, also found a significant (p<.01) agreement between Noble's m1 and the m values obtained from grade-school-aged subjects.

Successive Association: Another variant on the method of continued association is that of successive or intermittently repeated trials, in which the whole list of stimuli is presented several times, thereby separating each presentation of the stimulus by as many stimuli as there are in the total list. This is the standard method used for determining reproduction disturbances, in which case the subject is requested to repeat his response of the initial trial on the second trial. Appelbaum (1960) suggested expanding this technique to include a third trial on which the subject is requested to give a *new* response, the hypothesis being that by eliminating a highly over learned response it may be possible to see to what extent this stereotyped response masks some underlying thought disturbance. Milgram (1961) also has suggested that the reliance on highly over learned verbal habits may allow subjects to bypass idiosyncratic associative networks. The utility of this approach was borne out in a subsequent study (Appelbaum, 1960) in which brain-damaged subjects who were indistinguishable from nonbrain-damaged subjects on a reproduction test, showed more response disturbance and inability to produce a new response on the third trial. In a further study (Appelbaum, 1963) involving emotional stimuli, even though the subjects could be separated on the basis of second-trial reproduction responses, use of the third trial was a more effective differentiator.

A comparison of the standard reproduction test method with that proposed by Appelbaum indicated that reaction time on the critical trial is longer for the Appelbaum method, but that more errors are made when the standard method is used (Bodin & Geer, 1965).

The method of successive trials may be expanded to include studies in which there is a longer time interval between trials. Thus Weintraub, Silverstein, and Klee (1960), on retesting subjects after a 1-week interval, found the frequency of popular responses (responses which occurred with an absolute frequency of at least 10, in the Rapaport (Rapaport et. al., 1946) standardization data to significantly increase on the second test, while both association disturbances and reaction time significantly decreased. This finding was interpreted as reflecting a tendency of normal subjects to try to make more appropriate, adaptive responses to stressful stimuli, a hypothesis which finds some support in the fact that LSD subjects did not show this commonalty on a retest after a two-week interval, although 58% of the actual responses changed on the retest. However, as with LSD subjects, repeated testing of a group of schizophrenics over a 17-month period did not show any change in response commonalty.

S.S. Shapiro (1965), returning eighth-grade subjects on the same 30 stimuli 2 months later, similarly to Shakow, found that the number of Primary responses had increased, while 50% of the actual responses had changed on the retest. The Primary response increase was especially true for those subjects who learned, as a paired-associate task just prior to the second test, the Primary responses to eight of the WAT stimuli. However, it also occurred when the paired-associate task was administered.

Continued Association, Successive Trials: Two studies have combined the method of continued association with that of repeated trials. Kanungo and Lambert (1963) retested subjects on the same stimulus list after a 1-day interval and on a new stimulus list after a 2-day interval. In both cases, the number of relevant continued-association responses increased and the number of irrelevant responses decreased on the second test a finding which partially supports the Weintraub, et. al. hypothesis. In Jacob's study, (1959), subjects were required to write 10 responses to each of 13 neutral and emotional nouns, and were retested at an interval of 2 days, 1 week, or 2 months. For all time intervals, the proportion and rank of occurrence of identical responses on the second testing was significantly related to the order of elicitation of the response on the first presentation. Information on the absolute frequency of occurrence of Popular responses was not provided. Further studies of the effect of repeated trials on subsequent associative responses will be presented in the following section, in which type of preceding trial as a variable establishing psychological set will be discussed.

Continuous Association: The effect of continuous or chain association on subsequent associative responses has been studied by Osipow and Grooms (1965), who found that with successive links in the chain, strength of Primary response decreases, while number of different responses increases. Furthermore, the authors cite these findings of increased idiosyncrasy of response with increasing response links as support for Appelbaum's suggestion (1960) that investigating additional associative links might be clinically useful. Other continuous-association studies have been conducted by Cofer and Shevitz (1952) and Koen (1962), although the effect of the format of the test was not of concern in these investigations.

Additional Methods: Several other free-association methods have been proposed. One of these – that of discrete serial association – has been used by Fosmire (1965) to map the associative network of individual subjects. In this technique, the response to the first stimulus becomes the stimulus for the next trial; the second response, in turn, becomes the stimulus for the third trial; and so on. This technique is, then, similar to continuous association in that it elicits a chain of associative responses, but it differs in that there is more control over the actual stimulus for each link in the chain.

Another method of free association has been proposed by Robertson (1952). In this "time-limit version", the subject is instructed to write down as many words as possible within the time allotted. In addition, the subject is told that his responses must be phrases or sentences, and that one-word responses must be avoided. Twenty minutes is suggested as an optimal time limit.

Controlled Association

The other general format used to present stimuli is that of the restricted, or controlled, association test. In this case, the subject must choose his response from a restricted domain of responses specified by the experimenter. This domain may be determined by a semantic category (e.g., the response must be supraordinate to the stimulus) or by a particular concept (e.f., the response must be the name of a color). Alternatively, the domain may be restricted to a small number of response alternatives provided by the experimenter. A variant on this latter, multiple-choice association test is the Remote Associates Test (RAT) (S.A. Mednick, 1962; Wilson, Guilford, & Christensen, 1953), in which multiple stimuli are presented and the subject is restricted to a response which is associatively related to all the stimuli, This response may be forward or a reverse associate of the stimuli, In a related technique, Flaugher (1965) has made use of reverse association exclusively. Subjects are presented with an increasing number of associative responses and are requested to determine what stimulus word produced the given responses. In addition to the format of the RAT described above, Wilson et. al. (1953) also have suggested an alternate form in which the stimulus word is presented, followed by five letters. The subject must indicate which of the five is the first letter of the correct associative response.

In other controlled-association studies, responses may be restricted to a particular semantic class. The results of two studies in which subjects were restricted to a super- or subordinate responses (Peters, 1952, 1958) will be discussed below. An investigation in which the subjects were restricted to synonyms of the stimuli (Hills, 1958) is presented in Part II.

A study by Underwood and Richardson (1956) provides an example of controlled association in which the response concept category was specified. In this investigation, the method of simultaneous visual and oral presentation was used, and subjects were instructed to give sensory-impression responses. With practice and discussion, subjects were able to adopt this set successfully within approximately ten trials.

In another investigation in which response category was specified (Beck, 1960), approximately 1,000 teenage subjects were asked to respond with one of 11 colors to 60 WAT stimuli. The results indicated that only five of the stimulus words were not significantly associated with some color, and that no restricted subjects to "color" responses in a 10-minute continuous-association task and contrasted the performance on this production task with that on a task requiring the reproduction of a 40-item list of "food" words. The resulting responses were scored in terms of both a lenient and a rigid criterion. It was found that with increasing response restrictions (production versus reproduction; lenient versus rigid criterion) it was increasingly easy to differentiate among subject groups varying as to psychopathology. Bousfield and Barclay (1950) have also employed a continuous controlled-association task to determine the relationship between order and frequency of occurrence of a response. In this task, subjects were given 18 minutes to give as many "Bird", "Carpenter's Tools", or "Heavenly Bodies" responses as they could.

The use of the multiple-choice format, despite its expediency has thus far remained a less popular method. In one such study (Buchwalk, 1957), subjects were presented with the four response alternatives prior to being presented with the stimulus. Under these conditions, the obtained response frequencies were noted to differ (direction unspecified) from those obtained under discrete free-association conditions. The author hypothesizes that a recency effect may be responsible for this change. Priming studies to be reported subsequently would support his assumption. For example, Howes and Osgood (1954) found that the associative-response distributions to the same stimuli could be markedly altered by variations in the verbal context immediately preceding the stimulus word, and Storms (1958) noted that the presentation of an infrequent associative response just prior to the association test could increase significantly (that is, prime) the occurrence of that word as a response. These findings suggest that the overt presentation of response alternatives to the subject may produce a priming effect, whereby the usual distribution of associative responses is considerably changed.

It is clear that the use of a controlled-association test can substantially affect both the nature and frequency of the associative responses obtained.

Supplementary Reading

Cohen, R., & Swerdlik, M. (2009). *Psychological Testing and Assessment*. Ohio:McGraw-Hill Companies.
Aiken, L., & Groth-Marnat, G. (2005). Psychological Testing and Assessment (12th Edition) New Jersey:Allyn & Bacon.
Cohen, R. (2009). *Exercises in Psychological Testing and Assessment*. Ohio:McGraw-Hill Companies.
Urbina, S. (2004.) *Essentials of Psychological Testing*. New Jersey: John Wiley & Sons, Inc.
Stuart-Hamilton, I. (2007). *Dictionary of Psychological Testing, Assessment and Treatment*. Philadelphia: Jessica Kingsley Publishers.
Cohen, J. & Swerdlik, M. (2004). *Psychological Testing and Assessment: An Introduction to Tests and Measurement with Student Workbook*. California:Mayfield Publishing.

"A man never knows what he cannot do until he tries to undo what he did."
Unknown

Section 3
General Instructions for
Administering Tests

At the start, in order to establish proper motivation, read the following Introductory Remarks to the person being tested. Always make a point of asking the person what he wishes to be called and use his name frequently while testing. Also, tell him what you wish to be called.

INTRODUCTORY REMARKS:

"I'm going to ask you some quiz questions to see how you compare with others your same age. As we go along, the questions will become more difficult so don't get discouraged. Listen carefully and answer as many as you can. They are all to be done in your head and not with paper and pencil. If you are not sure of an answer, at least make a try. If you are certain that you don't know the answer, just say "PASS". There's no time limit so don't feel hurried. But please don't waste any time and don't ask if you are right or wrong for I'm not allowed to give you the answers. Now, let's start with this one."

If the person does not feel well, has a headache or cold, testing should not be attempted. The individual should always know why he is being tested, in simple but truthful terms – "for purposes of your guidance, in order to see that you take the right school program, to determine your strong as well as your weak points, to determine your potential ability, to help you do better work, etc."

The materials necessary for administering a test are listed in the front of the exam, or in the companion literature which comes with each testing tool.

The testing should be conducted in a quiet place, free from any distractions. It should be a comfortable room with good lighting and proper ventilation – not too warm and not too cold. You should be seated at a desk or table with the person being tested at your side in such a way that he, too, can use the desk. Do not tell the answers to the person being tested as this would spoil it for another testing period.

Many exams can be taken in group format, but most are given to but one person at a time. In this way, it overcomes some of the shortcomings of the group tests which are timed and unfairly penalize individuals who are ultra careful and methodical, fearful and easily upset under the pressure of speed, poorly motivated or uncooperative, or those who have reading handicaps or who misunderstand the importance of the task at hand and look out of the window when they should be making every second count.

The time required to give and score each test varies from about 10 to 15 minutes for some, to 3 hours for others. If the testing is started and cannot be completed because of lack of time, it can be continued another day or another week. However, it is always best to try to finish it at one sitting if possible.

After reading the INTRODUCTORY REMARKS to the person being tested, turn to the exam and begin testing. Follow instructions exactly.

Offer plenty of encouragement without giving any clues other than those contained in the test. Should an individual ask for further explanation of a question, reread the entire question as it appears in the text or reread parts of the question.

When the questions become difficult and a person seems to be a bit upset or discouraged, a word of encouragement can be most helpful.

If a test is not timed in any way, then specifically tell the person to take his time and not to hurry. In this way, a more accurate measure of intelligence, personality, etc. capacity is obtained.

It is important to be very fair in scoring the responses. We all have a bias, of course. Some people we like and others we don't. But in testing, try to be as unbiased as possible and show no favoritism.

HELPFUL CHECKLIST FOR TEST ADMINISTRATORS

Here are just a few ideas to help you in administering a test. As you start to test individuals, you will find that most tests are easy to administer. They have been specifically constructed so that professionals not familiar with prior testing situations can do so easily, thus allowing more individuals to receive the benefits of individualized testing.

1. Try to make the examinee feel as comfortable as possible. The testing environmental setting is important. It should be quiet, free from distractions, well lighted and properly ventilated.

2. You should feel generally poised. Facial and voice expressions should be relaxed. Be informal and relieve fear and tension by quickly getting at the job to be done.

3. Give yourself enough room; a good sized table on which to place both the manual and the score sheet is helpful.

4. Mark all questions clearly, and ensure that, if you are recording responses, you do so accurately.

5. If later on in the testing an examinee suddenly remembers an answer to a previous question, it is usually permissible to go back to the question. Check the administration of the test you are giving for guidance.

6. It is important to establish confidence with the examinee, so if the questions become too difficult and the subject seems upset, encourage them.

7. Testing may be continued at a later time or date if for some reason the testing environment is interrupted and you are not able to complete the testing in one sitting. However, it is always best to try to finish the testing in one sitting if possible.

8. If the examinee gives a wrong answer but then corrects himself, give credit. You can learn much about a person by watching their test taking behavior.

9. When asking items involving memory for numbers forwards or backwards, do not group the numbers in any way. The numbers should be asked in a monotonous manner – one number per second.

10. If the examinee's answer is ever in doubt, ask for a more detailed explanation.

11. If asking questions, make sure the examinee has heard the question correctly. It is always acceptable to repeat questions.

12. When asking vocabulary questions, you may spell the word out for the examinee. You should not use the word in any sentence other than the one offered in the test manual.

13. When answering vocabulary questions, the examinee may use the word in a sentence to explain the definition or grasp context.

14. The examinee is to do all the work in his head, unless otherwise specified.

15. It is permissible to give encouragement. It is acceptable to say, "now take your time" or "think before you answer". However, too much prodding or rephrasing of test questions will bias test results.

16. Try to make your delivery of instructions and questions smooth, read over and familiarize yourself with the questions beforehand.

17. Check your speed when asking questions. Your voice should be natural, not forced or stilted, and the speed should be even, neither too fast nor too slow.

18. Make sure you keep only score sheet or other paper you take notes on out of the field of vision of the examinee.

19. You may wish to type out the INTRODUCTORY REMARKS, rewording or emphasizing important parts in your own way, when special situations arise. An example of this might be testing a child with a partial hearing loss. In such a case, you might want to stress the importance of proper eye contact or lip movement.

Recommended Tests for Christian Counselors

ADMINISTERING THE DISC BEHAVIORAL PROFILE

The DISC Behavioral Profile is the questionnaire which the IACCP uses to collect the information needed in order to provide the counselor with a basic view of the person's behavioral style. When administering the Behavioral Profile, please insure that:

   a. The person being tested reads the instructions.

   b. The person does not analyze, i.e., take a lot of time deliberating. The test should only take about eight (8) minutes.

   c. No one else interprets what the questions mean. The person being tested must decide for himself/herself; this is part of the test.

   d. All questions are answered and legible.

   e. All requested information is printed on the front cover, including your name and the date.

Your cost is $10.00 each. This amount must accompany the test. Most ministers and professional counselors charge the counselee a minimum of $30.00 for this profile.

"Life is painting a picture, not doing a sum."
Justice O. W. Holmes

Section 4
Practical Wisdom

Life History Questionnaire

The purpose of this questionnaire is to obtain a comprehensive picture of your background. In scientific work, records are necessary since they permit a more thorough dealing with one's problems. By completing these questions as fully and as accurately as you can, you will facilitate your therapeutic program. You may be requested to answer these questions at home or perhaps start it in the waiting room. Your counselor/therapist will inform you.

It is understandable that you might be concerned about what happens to the information about you, because much or all of this information is highly personal. Case records are strictly confidential. No outsider is permitted to see your case record without your written permission.

If you do not desire to answer any questions, merely write "Do not care to answer".

Today's Date _____

1. General

Name _____

Address_____

Telephone (____)_____

Age_____ Occupation _____

_____

With whom are you now living? (list people) _____

_____

Do you live in a house, hotel, room, apartment, etc.?_____

Marital status: (circle answer)

Single   Engaged   Married   Remarried Separated

Divorced   Widowed

2. Clinical

   a. State in your own words the nature of your main
      problems and their duration.

   b. Give a brief account of the history and development of
      your complaints (from onset to present).

   c. On the scale below please estimate the severity of your
      problem(s):

      (mildly)   (moderately)   (very)   (extremely)   (totally

Upsetting)   (severe)   (severe severe)   (incapacitating)

d. Whom have you previously consulted about your present problem(s)?

3. Personal data

a. Date of birth _____ Place of birth _____

b. Mother's condition during pregnancy (as far as you know)

_____

c. Underline any of the following that applied during your childhood:

night terrors	bed-wetting	sleepwalking
thumb-sucking	nail-biting	stammering
fears	happy childhood	unhappy childhood

d. Health during childhood _____
list illnesses:

e. Health during adolescence _____
list illnesses:

117

f. What is your height?_____Your weight?_____

g. Any surgical operations? (Please list them and give age at time).

h. When were you last examined by a doctor?_____

i. Any accidents? _____

j. List your five main fears:

    1. _____

    2. _____

    3. _____

    4. _____

    5. _____

k. Circle any of the following that apply to you:

fatigue	insomnia	nightmares	Take sedatives
alcoholism	feel tense	feel panicky	tremors
depressed	suicidal ideas	take drugs	unable to relax

sexual problem	shy with people	don't like weekends/vacations	overambitious
can't make decisions	inferiority feeling	home conditions bad	can't make friends
memory problem	unable to have a good time	can't keep a job	concentration difficulties
financial problems			

others_____

1. Circle any of the following words which apply to you:

worthless	useless	a "nobody"	"life is empty"
inadequate	stupid	incompetent	Naïve
"can't do anything right"	guilty	evil	morally wrong
horrible thoughts	hostile	full of hate	anxious
agitated	cowardly	unassertive	panicky
aggressive	ugly	deformed	unattractive
repulsive	depressed	lonely	unloved
misunderstood	bored	restless	confused
unconfident	in conflict	full of regrets	worthwhile
sympathetic	intelligent	attractive	confident
considerate			

others _____

m. Present interests, hobbies, and activities:

n. How is most of your free time occupied?

o. What is the last grade of schooling that you completed?

_____

p. Scholastic abilities – strengths and weaknesses:

q. Do you make friends easily? _____

Do you keep them? _____

4. Occupational data

a. What sort of work are you doing now?

b. Kinds of jobs held in the past?

c. Does your present work satisfy you? (If not, in what ways are you dissatisfied?)

d. Ambitions:

past:

present:

5. Sex information

    a. parental attitudes to sex (i.e., was there sex instruction or discussion in the home?)

    b. When and how did you acquire your first knowledge of sex?

    c. When did you first become aware of your own sexual impulses?

    d. Did you ever experience any anxieties or guilt feelings arising out of sex or masturbation? If "yes", please explain.

    e. Any relevant details regarding your first or subsequent sexual experience?

    f. Is your present sex life satisfactory? (If not, please explain).

    g. Provide information about any significant heterosexual and/or homosexual reactions:

6. Marital history

a. How long have you been married? _____

b. How long did you know your marriage partner before engagement? _____

c. Husband's/wife's age_____

d. Occupation of husband or wife _____

e. Personality of husband or wife (in your own words):

f. In what areas is there compatibility?

g. In what areas is there incompatibility?

h. How do you get along with your in-laws? (This includes brothers and sisters-in-laws).

i. How many children do you have? _____

   Please list their sex and age(s):

j. Any relevant details regarding miscarriages or abortions?

k. Give details of any previous marriage(s):

1. Personality of each child (in your own words):

7. Family data

   a. Father:

      Living or deceased? _____

      If deceased, your age at the time of his death? _____

      Cause of death_____

      If alive, father's present age_____

      Occupation_____

   b. Mother:

      Living or deceased? _____

      If deceased, your age at the time of her death? _____

      Cause of death_____

      If alive, mother's present age_____

      Occupation_____

   c. Siblings:

      number of brothers' _____ brother's ages _____

      number of sisters' _____ sister's ages_____

relationship with siblings:

past:

present:

Give a description of your father's personality and his attitude toward you (past and present):

Give a description of your mother's personality and her attitude toward you (past and present):

In what ways were you punished by your parents as a child?

Give an impression of your home atmosphere (i.e., the home which you grew up. Mention state of compatibility between parents and between parents and children).

Were you able to confide in your parents? _____

If you have a step-parent, give your age when parent remarried?_____

Give an outline of your religious training:

If you were not brought up by your parents, who did bring you up and between what years?

Has anyone (parents, relatives, friends) ever interfered in your life? How?

Who are the most important people in your life?:

Does any member of your family suffer from alcoholism, epilepsy or anything which can be considered a "mental disorder"? Give details.

Are there any other members of the family about whom information regarding illness, etc. is relevant?

Recount any fearful or distressing experiences not previously mentioned:

List any situations that make you feel particularly anxious:

List the benefits you hope to derive from counseling:

List any situations which make you feel calm or relaxed:

Have you ever lost control (i.e., temper or crying or aggression)? If so, please describe.

Please add any information not covered by this questionnaire that may aid your counselor in understanding and helping you.

Use the rest of this page and the attached blank page to give a word picture of your self as you would be described:

  a.   by yourself.

  b.   by your spouse (if married).

  c.   by your best friend.

  d.   by someone who dislikes you.

Pick two words from each list that best describe how you see yourself. I feel (temporary) or I am (more permanent).

List #1	List #2	List #3
happy	confused	sensitive
friendly	shaky	impulsive
sad	confident	authentic
lonely	poised	intelligent
depressed	nervous	anxious
guilty	wondering	responsible
justified	dreamy	arrogant
upset	adventurous	suspicious
tired	dominant	inferior
above	exploited	mysterious
silly	jealous	insignificant
scared	frustrated	imitative
uptight	doubtful	courageous
stopped	angry	immoral
open	honest	unpredictable
closed	passive	unstable
secure	energetic	depressed
excited	embarrassed	aware
alone	fearful	virtuous
bitchy	together	suffering
	peaceful	growing
	defeated	ambitious
	accepting	submissive
	hopeful	fulfilled
	forgiving	unworthy
	insecure	withdrawn
	satisfied	

COUNSELING REPORT

EVALUATION

Name: Address:

Phone: Age:

Reason for Referral:

Church Affiliation: Home Fellowship:

Date Started Counseling:

Date of Report:

Relevant Social and Diagnostic History

Behavioral Observations and Impressions

Test Results and Interpretation

<u>Counseling Goals</u>

1. Attempted

2. Accomplished

<u>**Summary and Recommendations**</u>

Supervisors Evaluation and Recommendation

_____

Counselor

_____

Supervisors Signature

_____

Date

Case Notes

Client Name: C and H C   Date of Service: 3/9/00

Address: 1234 Heaven Lane   Phone: 555-555-5555
Any ware, USA   DOB: na

Presenting Problem

C and H referred by their pastor for marital counseling. They have a 6 year old son and want to be better partners and also better parents.

History

They have been married for 12 years. C is the son of a business family which showed very little affection; he is spoiled, having always been bailed out by his parents. He owns Card shop. About 6 years ago, he had an emotional affair, which H has not forgiven. She is in the legal profession, with an ingenious style, a bit cutesy and histrionic, co-dependent. She states she just wants to be treated with higher priority, and wants to have better communication.

Dynamics

They lack healthy communication; he sees her as mother figure to rescue and fix things for him. He is characterized as a mama's boy, developmentally delayed (EI). He has expressed intense rage, especially during his breakdown. He sees himself as a victim. She sees him as the rejecting and demanding father; she is filled with much anger, fear, hurt, unforgiveness bordering on bitterness. Very passive aggressive in style.

Summary and Treatment

My hope is to see better communication, resolving of problems, and the reduction of significant deficits in each.

Section 5
Frequently Asked
Questions and Answers On
Psychological Tests
And
Measurements

Question:
1. What did Esquirol and Sequin contribute to the development of psychological test?

Answer:
The French physician Esquirol contributed what is probably the first explicit two volume work published in 1838, in which over one hundred pages are devoted to mental retardation. Esquirol also pointed out that there are many degrees of mental retardation, varying along a continuum from normality to "low-grade idiocy". In trying to develop a system for classifying the different degrees and varieties of retardation, he tried several procedures but concluded that the individual's use of language provides the most dependable criterion of his or her intellectual level. It is interesting to note that current criteria of mental retardation are also largely linguistic and that present day intelligence tests are heavily loaded with verbal content.

Sequin (1866-1907) pioneered in the training of the mentally retarded. He rejected the accepted notion at the time of the insurability of mental retarded. Severely retarded children are given intensive exercise in sensory discrimination and in the development of motor control using these methods. Some of the procedures developed by Sequin for this purpose were eventually incorporated into performance or nonverbal tests of intelligence. An example is the Sequin Form Board, in which the individual is required to insert variously shaped blocks into the corresponding recesses as quickly as possible.

Question:
   2. Describe Army Alpha and Army Beta test.

Answer:
Group testing, like the Binet scale, was developed to meet a pressing practical need. When the United States entered World War I in 1917, a committee was developed to see if psychology might assist in the conduct of the war. This committee, under the direction of Robert M. Yerkes, recognized the need for the rapid classification of the million and a half recruits with respect to general intellectual level. The army psychologists drew on all available test materials, especially on an unpublished group intelligence test prepared by Arthur S. Otis. The test that was finally developed by the army psychologists came to be known as the Army Alpha and the Army Beta. The former was designed for general routine testing; the latter was a non language scale used to test illiterates and foreign born recruits who were unable to take a test in English. Both tests were suitable for administration to large groups and served as models for most group intelligence tests.

Question:
   3. Define "Mental Test".

Answer:
Definition: Mental test was used for the first time by James McKeen Cattell in an article he wrote in 1890. Described in this article was a series of tests that were being administered

annually to college students in an effort to determine their intellectual level. These tests were administered individually. They measured muscular strength, speed of movement, sensitivity to pain, keenness of vision and of hearing, weight discrimination, reaction to time, memory and the like.

Question:
    4. What did Alfred Binet do?

Answer:
Alfred Binet more than half a century after the work of Esquirol and Sequin urged that children who failed to respond to normal schooling be examined before dismissal and if considered educable, be assigned to special classes. Binet stimulated the Ministry of Public Instruction to take steps to improve the condition of retarded children. A specific outcome was the establishment of a ministerial commission for the study of retarded children, to which Binet was appointed. In 1904, the Ministry of Public Instruction appointed Binet to the previously cited commission to study procedures for the education of retarded children. It was in connection with the objectives of this commission that Binet, in collaboration with Simon, prepared the first Binet-Simon Scale, (Binet & Simon, 1905).

Concerns & Issues on Psychological Testing

Question:
    5. Define behavior sample.

Answer:
Definition: Behavior sample is a sample of behavior that is psychologically tested in an objective and standardized manner. Observations are made on a small carefully chosen sample of an individual's behavior. The psychologist proceeds in much the

same way as the biochemist who tests a patient's blood or a community's water supply by analyzing one or more samples of it.

Question:
6. Define standardization.

Answer:
Definition: Standardization implies unity of procedure in administering and scoring the test. When comparing the test results of different people the testing conditions must be the same for all. This requirement is needed in all scientific observations because it provides controlled conditions. In a test situation, the distinct variable is often the individual being tested. The test instructor in order to provide uniformity of testing conditions, provides precise directions for administering each newly developed test. A major part of standardizing a new test is the formulation of the directions.

The establishment of "norms" is an important step in standardization of a test. "Norms" are established by selecting a large group of people which represent the type of persons the test is designed for.

Question:
7. Discuss why the use of a psychological test should be controlled.

Answer:
There are two important reasons for controlling the use of psychological test. (1) to assure that the test is used by a qualified examiner; and (2) to prevent general knowledge of the test content, which would invalidate the test. A qualified examiner is needed in each of these three major testing

situations; selection of the test, administration of the test and scoring and the interpretation of the scores. In order to forestall deliberate efforts to fake scores, test content definitely has to be restricted.

Question:
8. Discuss basic issues in test administration.

Answer:
Advance preparation is the most single important requirement for good testing procedure. Being totally familiar with the specific testing procedure is another important consideration in both individual and group testing. For individual testing, it is usually required to have supervised training in the administration of a particular test. For group testing and especially in large scale projects, the preparation may include advance briefing of examiners and proctors, so that each is fully familiar with the function he or she is to perform. The proctors hand out and collect test materials and make certain that instructions are followed.

Standardized procedure applies timing, materials and testing surroundings. A suitable testing room should be selected, free from noise and distractions; adequate lightning, ventilation, seating facilities, and space for the test takers. Special steps should also be taken to prevent interruptions from happening while the testing is being done. These may include putting a sign on the door to indicate that a test is in progress, or when testing a large group, locking the doors or stationing someone outside each door is effective in preventing the entrance of late-comers.

Question:
9. Discuss test anxiety.

Answer:

It is possible that if students have performed poorly on previous tests that they may develop test anxiety, having experienced failure and frustration in previous test situations. Supporting this interpretation are the findings that within subgroups of high scores on intelligence tests, the negative correlation between anxiety levels and test performance disappeared. There is also evidence suggesting that at least some of the relationship results from the destructive effects of anxiety on test performance. In one study, (Waite, Sarason, Lighthall, & Davidson, 1958) high anxious and low anxious children coequaled in intelligence test scores were given repeated trails in a learning task. Although initially equal in the learning test, the low anxious group improved significantly more than the high-anxious group.

Two important components have been identified with regard to the nature of test anxiety, namely, emotionality and worry. Feelings and physiological reactions such as tension and increasing heartbeat comprises the emotional component. The worry or cognitive component includes negative self-oriented thoughts, such as expectation of doing poorly and concern about the consequences of failure. These thoughts draw attention away from the task-oriented behavior required by the test and thereby disrupt performance.

Question:
10. Discuss how training may affect test performance.

Answer:

In evaluating the effects of training or practice on test scores, it becomes obvious that any educational experience the individual undergoes, either formal or informal, in or out of school should be reflected in her or his performance on tests that sample the relevant aspects of behavior. It is obvious also that the closer the resemblance between test content and coaching material, the greater will be the improvement in test scores. Coaching in the more traditional sense, is designed to develop skills that are confined and of very little use in life activities. Beside the practice of "teaching to the test" tends to center on the particular sample of skills and knowledge covered by the test, rather than the broader knowledge range that the test tries to judge. Donlon, 1684; Messick, 1980, 1981 Messick and Jungeblut, 1981; these studies covered an assortment of coaching methods and included students from both public and private schools and minority students from both urban and rural areas. The end result from these studies is that intensive drill on items similar to those on the SAT is unlikely to show an appreciable gain than occurs when students are retested with the SAT after a year of regular high school instruction. Effective training in broadly applicable cognitive skills should improve the trainee's ability to cope with ensuing intellectual task. Test performance desired goals are enhanced when both test scores and criterion performance are improved even though the test validity is unchanged.

Question:
11. Briefly discuss the social and ethical considerations in testing.

Answer:
Assessment Techniques is one of the Ethical Principles specifically directed to testing. It is concerned with the development, publication and use of psychological assessment techniques. Another of these is Competence, this is especially relevant to potential misuses of tests by unqualified users. It states that psychologists "only provide services and experience". Still another principle, confidentiality, although wider in scope,

is also highly relevant to testing, the same as parts of most of the other principles. One way to protect the test taker against the improper use of the test is to have as a requirement that the test be given only by appropriately qualified examiners. The necessary qualifications vary with the type of test. A long period of thorough training and supervised experience is necessary for the proper implementation of individual intelligence tests and most personality tests. For the educational achievement or job proficiency tests, only a minimum of specialized psychological training is needed. It is important to point out that students who take tests in class for instructional purposes are not as a rule qualified to administer the tests to others or explain the scores properly.

The purchase of tests is generally restricted to persons who meet certain minimal qualifications. The effort to restrict the distribution of tests serves two purposes: security of test materials and prevention of misuse. The sincere efforts that the tests distributors make to implement these objectives is limited.

Statistics in Testing
Brief Overview

Question:
12. Describe central tendencies and variability's.

Answer:
The height of the column erected over each class interval corresponds to the number of persons scoring in that interval in the histogram. In a frequency polygon, the number of persons in each interval is indicated by a point place in the center of the class interval and across from the appropriate frequency. The successive points are then joined by straight lines.

A group of scores can be described in terms of some measure of central tendency. Such a measure provides a single, most typical or representative score to characterize the performance of the entire group. The most familiar of these that we know is called the average or the "mean" (M). The mean is found by adding all scores and dividing the sum by the number of cases. Another measure of central tendency is the mode, or the most frequent score.

The mode is the midpoint of the class interval with the highest frequency in a frequency distribution. A third measure of central tendency is the median, or middlemost score when all scores have been arranged in order of size. The median is the point that divides the distribution, half the cases above it and half below it.

Question:
    13. Discuss developmental norms.

Answer:
A way in which significance can be attached to test scores is to indicate how far along the normal developmental path the individual has progressed. For instance, let's take an 8 year old who takes an intelligence test and performs as well as a 10 year old. This would also hold true for a mentally retarded adult who performed at the same level. They also would be assigned a MA of 10. Mental age norms have been employed with tests that are not divided into levels. In this instance a child's raw score is first determined. These scores can be taken any number of ways. It may be the total number of correct items on the whole test, or it may be based on time, on the number of errors or it could be a combination of these. To sum it all up, ordinal scales are designed to identify the stage reached by the child in the development of specific behavior functions. Age level scores are

secondary to a qualitative description of the child's characteristic behavior. The order of such scales shows the uniform progression of development through successive stages. Even though these scales provide information about what a child is actually able to do, they also share some important features with the criterion-reference tests.

Question:
14. Discuss within-group norms.

Answer:
Mostly all standardized tests provide some form of within-group norms. The individual's performance is evaluated in terms of the performance of the most nearly comparable standardization group, as when comparing a child's raw score with that of children of the same chronological age or in the same school grade. Within-group scores have a uniform and clearly defined quantitative significance and can be appropriately applied in most types of statistical examination.

The percentile score is the way we determine if one falls in the norm. A percentile indicates the individual's relative position in the standardization sample. Percentile scores are expressed in terms of the percentage of persons in the standardization sample who fall below a given raw score. An example of this would be that if 28% of the people obtain fewer than 15 problems correct on a math reasoning test, than the raw score of 15 corresponds to the 28th percentile. Percentiles can also be regarded as ranks in a group of 100, except that in ranking, it is accustomed to start at the top, so that the best person in the group is rated as one. On the other hand with percentiles, we begin at the bottom, so that the lower the percentile, the lower the individual's standing. The 50th percentile corresponds to the median. Percentiles above 50 represent average performance;

those below, represent below average performance.

<u>Question:</u>
   15. What do we mean by criterion referenced testing?

<u>Answer:</u>
In the 1970s an approach to testing that aroused a surge of activity, especially in education, had been designated as "criterion-referenced testing". First proposed by Glaser, this term is still used somewhat loosely and it's definition varies among different writers. A specific content is the framework of this type of testing. In criterion-referenced testing, for example, a test takers performance may be reported in terms of the specific kinds of math operations he or she has mastered, the estimated size of his or her vocabulary, the difficulty level of reading matter he or she can comprehend, or the chances of his or her achieving a designated performance level on an external criterion.

The distinguishing feature of criterion-referenced testing is its interpretation of test performance in terms of content meaning. The focus here is clearly on what test takers can do and what they know, not on how they compare with others. A fundamental requirement in constructing this type of test is a clearly defined domain of knowledge or skills to be assessed by the test. If scores on such a test are to have communicable meaning, the content domain to be sampled must be widely recognized as important. A second major feature associated with criterion-reference testing is the procedure of testing for mastery. Basically, this procedure yields an all or nothing score, indicating that the individual has or has not attained the preestablished level or mastery. When basic skills are tested, nearly complete mastery is generally expected.

Question:
   16. Name different types of reliability measure and discuss
       split-half and Kuder-Richardson.

Answer:
Test-Retest Reliability.
The most obvious method for finding the reliability of test scores
is by repeating the identical test on a second occasion. The
reliability coefficient in this case is simply the correlation
between the scores obtained by the same persons on the two
administrations of the test. The random fluctuations of
performance from one test session to another corresponds to the
variance in errors. These variations may result in part from
uncontrolled testing conditions, such as extreme changes in
weather, sudden noises and other distractions. They also arise
from changes in the test takers themselves, as depicted by
illness, fatigue, emotional strain, worry, and recent experience of
a pleasant or unpleasant nature. The higher the reliability, the
less susceptible the scores are to random changing, either by the
test taker or the testing environment.

Alternative-Form Reliability
One way to avoid the difficulties encountered in test retest
reliability is through the use of alternative forms of the test.
This way the same person can be tested with one form on the
first occasion and with another alternate form on the second.
The parallel between the scores obtained on the two forms
represents the reliability coefficient of the rest.

Split-Half Reliability
By dividing the test into equivalent halves, two scores are
obtained for each person, From a single administration of one
form of a test, it is possible to arrive at a measure of reliability
by various split-half procedures. It is apparent that split-half

reliability provides a measure of consistency with regard to content sampling. Temporal stability of the scores does not enter into such reliability, because only one test session is involved. This type of reliability coefficient is sometimes called a coefficient of internal consistency, since only a single administration of a single form is required. Kuder-Richardson Reliability and Coefficient Alpha is another method for finding reliability. Utilizing a single administration of a single form it is based on the consistency of responses to all items in the test. This interim consistency is influenced by two sources of error variance: (1) content sampling and (2) heterogeneity of the behavior domain sampled. The more consistent the domain, the higher the interim consistency. An example of this would be that if one test includes only multiplication, while another consists of addition, subtraction, multiplication and division the former test will probably show more interim consistency then the latter. The most common procedure for finding interim consistency is that developed by Kuder and Richardson. Interim consistency is found from a single administration of a single test the same as in the split half method. Instead of requiring two half scores, however, this technique is based on an examination of performance on each item.

Question:
  17. Define Standard Error of Measurement.

Answer:
The reliability of a test may be expressed in terms of the standard error of measurement (SEM). For many testing purposes, it is therefore more useful than the reliability coefficient. The standard error of measurement can be easily computed from the reliability coefficient of the test.

It is especially important to consider test reliability and errors of measurement when evaluating the differences between two scores. Thinking in terms of the range within which each score may fluctuate serves as a check against over emphasizing small differences between scores.

Question:
    18. Discuss content-related validation.

Answer:
Content-related validation involves essentially the systematic examination of the test content to determine whether it covers a representative sample of the behavior domain to be measured. Such a validation procedure is commonly used in evaluating achievement test. This type of test is designed to measure how well the individual has mastered a specific skill or course of study. Content validity is built into a test from the outset through the choice of appropriate items. For educational tests, the preparation of items is preceded by a thorough systematic examination of relevant course syllabi and textbooks, as well as by consultation with subject-matter experts. On the basis of the information thus gathered, test specifications are drawn up for the item writers. These specifications should show the content areas or topics to be covered, the instructional objectives or processes to be tested, and the relative importance of individual topics and processes.

Question:
    19. Discuss criterion-related validation.

Answer:
Criterion-related procedures indicate the effectiveness of a test in predicting an individual's performance in specified activities. For this purpose, performance on the test is checked against a criterion, that is, a direct and independent measure of that

which the test is designed to predict. Thus, for a mechanical aptitude test, the criterion might be subsequent job performance as a machinist; for a scholastic aptitude test, it might be collegiate grades; and for a neuroticism test, it might be associates ratings or other available information regarding the individual's behavior in various life situations.

Question:
20. Discuss construct-related validation.

Answer:
The construct-related validity of a test is the extent to which the test may be said to measure a theoretical construction or trait. Scholastic aptitude, mechanical comprehension, verbal fluency, speed of walking, neuroticism and anxiety are some examples of such constructs. Each construct is developed to explain and organize observed response consistencies. Age differentiation is a major criterion used in the validation of a number of traditional intelligence tests. Most pre-school tests as well as the Stanford-Binet test are checked against chronological age to determine whether the scores show a progressive increase with advancing age.

This term "construct validity" was introduced into the psychometrist's dictionary in 1954 in the Technical Recommendations for Psychological Tests and Diagnostic Techniques, which constitutes the first edition of the 1985 testing standards. The theoretical construct, trait, or behavior range measured by a particular test can be amply defined only in the light of documentation gathered in that test. Such a definition should take into account the variables with which the test correlated significantly, as well as the conditions found to affect its scores and the groups that differ significantly in such scores.

Recognized that the development of a valid test requires multiple procedures, which are employed gradually, at different stages of test construction. Validity is therefore built into the test from the beginning, rather then being limited to the last stages of test development, as in traditional criterion-related validation. The validation process begins with the formulation of detailed characteristic or compose definitions, derived from psychological theory, prior research, or systematic observation and analyses of the relevant behavior range. Test items are then prepared to fit the construct definitions. Experimental item analyses follow, with the selection of the most effective, or valid, items from the initial item pools. Other appropriate internal analyses may then be carried out, including statistical analyses of items clusters of subtests. The final stage includes validation of various scores and interpretative combinations of scores through statistical analyses against external, real-life criteria.

Question:
21. Discuss item difficulty.

Answer:
The difficulty of an item is defined in terms of the percentage of persons who answer it correctly. For instance, the easier the item, the larger will be this percentage. It is therefore customary to arrange items in order of difficulty, so that test takers begin with relatively easy items and proceed to items of increasing difficulty. This arrangement gives the test taker confidence in approaching the test and also reduces the likelihood of their wasting too much time on items beyond their ability while neglecting the easier items that they can complete correctly.

The percentage of persons skipping an item will express item difficulty in terms of an original scale. It correctly indicates the rank order or relative difficulty of items. For example, if items 1, 2 and 3 are passed by 30%, 20%, and 10% of the cases, respectively, we can conclude that item 1 is the easiest and item 3 is the hardest of the three.

Question:
   22. Discuss item discrimination.

Answer:
This refers to the degree to which an item differentiates correctly among test takers in the behavior that the test is designated to measure. Then the test as a whole is to be evaluated by means of criterion-related validation, the items may themselves be evaluated and selected on the basis of their relationship to the same external criterion. This procedure has been followed especially in the development of certain personality generally followed in choosing items for inclusion to biographical inventories, which typically cover a heterogeneous collection of background facts about the individual.

Question:
   23. Discuss how speeded tests are item-analyzed.

Answer:
Whether or not speed is relevant to the function being measured, item indices computed from a speeded test may be misleading. Except for items that all or nearly all examinees have had time to attempt, the time indices found from a speed test will reflect the position of the item in the test rather than its inbred difficulty or discriminative power. Items that appear late in the test will be passed by a relatively small percentage of the total sample, because a few persons have time to reach these items. Regardless of how easy the item may be, if it appears late in a speeded test, it will appear difficult. Even if the question was to merely asked for one's name, the percentage of persons

who passed it might be very low if the item were placed toward the end of the speeded test. This was later proven when comparable groups of high school students were given two forms of verbal test and two forms of a mathematics test. Each of the two forms contained the same items as the other, but the item occurring early in one form was placed late in the other. Each form was administered with a short time limit and with a very liberal time limit. Various inter comparisons were therefore possible between forms and timing conditions. The results clearly showed that the position of an item in the speeded tests affected its indices of difficulty and discrimination. When the same item occurred later in a speed test, it was passed by a greater percentage of those attempting it, and it yielded a higher item-criterion correlation.

Question:
24. Discuss cross-validation.

Answer:
It is essential that test validity be computed on a different sample of persons from that on which the items were selected. This independent determination of the validity of the entire test is known as cross-validation. Any validity co-efficient computed on the same sample that was used for item-selection purposes will capitalize on random sampling errors within that particular sample and will therefore be deceptively high.

Following is an example of cross-validation: let us suppose that out of sample of 100 medical students, the 30 with the highest and the 30 with the lowest medical school grades have been chosen to represent contrasted criterion groups. If now, these two groups are compared in a number of traits actually irrelevant to success in medical school, certain chance differences will undoubtedly be found. Therefore, there might be an excess of private school graduates and of red-haired persons within the upper criterion group. If we were to assign each individual a score by crediting her or him with one point for private school graduation and one point for red-hair, the means of such scores would undoubtedly be higher in the upper than in the lower criterion group.

Sample Tests Discussed: I.Q.

Question:
25. Compare Stanford-Binet Intelligence Scale with Wechsler Scale for Adults.

Answer:
The intelligence scales developed by David Wechsler include several successive editions of three scales, one designed for adults, one for school-age children and one for preschool children. Besides their use as a measure of general intelligence, the Wechslcr scales have been investigated as a possible aide in psychiatric diagnosis.

Tests were designed to cover a wide variety of functions, with special emphasis on judgment, comprehension, and reasoning, which Binet regarded as essential components of intelligence. Although sensory and perceptual tests were included, a much greater proportion of verbal content was found in this scale then in most test series of the time.

In 1904, the Minister of Public Instruction appointed Binet to the previously cited commission to study procedures for the education of retarded children. It was in connection with the objectives of this commission that Binet, in collaboration with Simon, prepared the first Binet-Simon scale (Binet & Simon, 1905).

Question:
   26. Discuss assessment of competence.

Answer:
Intelligence tests while individually administered by specially trained examiners are sometimes interpreted in a hasty and routine manner. Taking IQ's at face value in classifying children, for example, may lead to incorrect conclusions in the absence of the needed supplementary observations and background data. This approach to testing has sometimes been designated as the assessment of competence. It focuses on the knowledge, skills, and attitudes the individual can utilize to function effectively in specified environments and situations. A specific effort to bridge the gap between mass testing and individual assessment, with particular reference to the testing of cultural minorities, is illustrated by the work of Mercer. Mercer's long term research project led to the development of the System of Multicultural Pluralistic Assessment better known as SOMPA. Mercer was particularly concerned about the misclassification of children from culturally and linguistically diverse backgrounds as mentally retarded simply on the basis of intelligence test scores. SOMPA is a comprehensive assessment program, suitable for ages 5 to 11, which includes the WISC together with other standardized measures and supplementary data about the child's physical condition and social competence within his or her own environment.   The data-gathering procedure utilized in SOMPA include a one hour parent interview and an individual examination of the child, conducted over two or more testing sessions. SOMPA combines data from three separate assessment models, designated as medical, social system, and pluralistic models. Also included is the Bender-Visual Motor Gestalt Test, a clinical instrument widely used to assess perceptual motor development and to detect possible neurological impairment.

Question:
27. Discuss Bayley Scales of Infant Development.

Answer:
A well constructed test for the measurement of the earliest age levels of the Bayley Scales of Infant Development. These scales represent the end product of many years of research by Bayley and her co-workers, including the longitudinal investigations of the Berkeley Growth Study.

Question:
28. Discuss cross-cultural testing.

Answer:
A well constructed instrument for the pre-school level is the McCarthy Scales of Children Abilities. This is used for children between the ages of 2 ½ and 8 ½ years. It consists of 18 tests, grouped into six overlapping scales such as Verbal, Perceptual-Performance, Quantitative, General Cognitive, Memory, and Motor.

Question:
29. Discuss McCarthy Scales of Children Abilities.

Answer:
During the turn of the century large number of immigrants coming to the United States necessitated the development of some of the earliest cross-cultural tests. Other early tests originated in initial research on the comparative abilities of relatively isolated cultural groups. These cultures were often quite isolated and had little or no contact with Western, technologically advanced societies within whose framework most psychological tests had been developed. Traditionally, cross-cultural tests have tried to rule out one or more parameters with

which cultures differ. An example of this is language. Tests were developed that required no language on the part of the examiner or the test taker. Reading was ruled out when the educational backgrounds differed widely and illiteracy was common.

Question:
    30. Discuss the advantages and disadvantages of group testing.

Answer:
Mass testing began during World War I with the development of the Army Alpha and the Army Beta for use in the United States Army. Group tests are used primarily in the educational systems, government services, industry and the military services. The Army Alpha and Army Beta was a verbal test designed for general screening and placement purposes. Group tests are primarily designed as instruments for mass testing. An advantage of group testing is that it facilitates mass testing by greatly simplifying the examiner's role, in comparison to the extensive training and experience required to administer the Stanford-Binet. Scoring is typically more objective in group testing and can be done by a clerk. Most group tests can also be scored by computers. The disadvantages of group testing have been in the area of restrictions imposed on the examinee's responses. Another is the lack of flexibility.

Question:
    31. Define Multi-level Batteries

Answer:
To provide comparable measures of intellectual development over a broader range, series of overlapping multi-level batteries have been constructed. They are especially suitable for use in

schools, where comparability of scores over several years is desirable. For this reason the levels are typically described in terms of grades. Most multi-level batteries provide a reasonable degree of continuity with regard to content or intellectual functions covered.

Question:
32. Discuss stability-instability issue of I.Q.

Answer:
The intelligence test performance is quite stable as shown by the extensive body of data that has been accumulated over the elementary, high school, and college period. The effects of age and retest interval on retest correlations exhibit considerable regularity and are themselves highly predictable. One explanation for the increasing stability of the IT with age is provided by the cumulative nature of intellectual development. The individual's intellectual skills and knowledge at each age include all his or her earlier skills and knowledge plus an increment of new acquisitions. A second condition contributing to the general stability of the IQ pertains to the role of prerequisite learning skills on subsequent learning. Not only does the individual retain prior learning but much of her or his prior learning provides tools for subsequent learning. Hence the more progress a child has made in the acquisition of intellectual skills and knowledge at any one point in time, the better able he or she is to profit from subsequent learning experiences.

Studies of individuals on the other hand have shown instability of the IQ by the revealing of large upward or downward shifts in IQ. Sharp rises or drops in IQ may occur as a result of major environmental changes in the child's life. Such changes as the family structure or home conditions, adoption into a foster home, severe or prolonged illness and therapeutic or remedial programs are examples of events that may alter a child's following intellectual development. Research on the factors connected with increases and decreases in IQ throws light on the conditions determining intellectual development in general. The ability to predict subsequent intellectual status can be improved if measurements of the individual's emotional and motivational characteristics and also their environment are combined with initial test scores.

Question:
33. Discuss multiple-factor theories.

Answer:
The accepted modern American view of trait organization recognizes a number of moderately broad group factors, each of which may enter with different weights into different tests. For instance a verbal factor may have a large weight in a vocabulary test, a smaller weight in a verbal analogies test, and a still smaller weight in an arithmetic reasoning test. The distinction between general, group, and specific factors is not so basic as it may first appear. If the number of change of tests in a battery is small, a single general agent may account for all the correlations among them. But when the same tests are included in a larger battery with a more complete collection of tests, the original general agent may emerge as a group factor common to some but not all tests.

Question:
34. Define creativity and discuss its measurement.

Answer:
Studies of scientific talent became increasingly concerned with creative abilities. Interest shifted from the individual who is merely a dependable, accurate, and critical thinker to the one who also displays ingenuity, originality, and inventiveness.

Therefore, creativity, long regarded as the prime quality in artistic production, came to be widely known as a basis for scientific achievement as well.

Homogenous tests of creative aptitudes have been produced mainly in the course of research on the nature or development of creativity. The items in the creativity tests are usually open-ended, therefore precluding detached scoring. For this reason, it is essential to certify scorer reliability for all such instruments.

Aptitude Tests

Question:
   35. Briefly discuss special aptitude tests.

Answer:
It was generally recognized that intelligence tests were limited in their coverage of abilities even prior to the development of multiple aptitude batteries. Special aptitude tests were soon made in an effort to fill in the major gaps. Among the earliest they were designed to measure mechanical aptitude. Because traditional intelligence tests focus mainly on isolated functions involving the use of verbal or numeral symbols, a particular need was felt for tests covering the more concrete or practical abilities. Mechanical aptitude tests were developed in part to meet this need. The demands of occupational selection and counseling likewise stimulated the development of tests to measure special, clerical, musical, and artistic aptitudes. Tests of vision, hearing, and motor dexterity have also been widely utilized in the selection of classification of personnel for industrial and military purpose. A strong impetus to the construction of all special aptitude tests has been provided by the urgent problems of matching job requirements with the specific pattern of abilities characterizing each individuals.

Special Aptitude Test Cover Four Major Areas:

A. Psychomotor Skills are to measure speed, coordination, and other characteristics of movement responses.
B. Mechanical Aptitude tests cover a variety of functions. Psychomotor factors enter into some of the tests in this category, either because the rapid manipulation of materials is required in the performance of the tests, or because special subtests designed to measure motor dexterity are included in a paper and pencil test. Mechanical reasoning and sheer mechanical information predominate in a number of mechanical aptitude tests.
C. Clerical Aptitudes are designed to measure clerical aptitudes characterized by a common emphasis on perceptual speed. They are designed also primarily for such purposes as the counseling or selection of potential trainees, or the assignment of present employees to newly established computer functions within an office.
D. Testing in the Professions, examination covers both facts and methodology of psychology; it also requires being familiar with the Ethical Principles of Psychologists and with appropriate professional, governmental, and judicial guidelines and regulations.

Question:
   36. Discuss career counseling.

Answer:
Several multiple aptitude batteries have been incorporated in

career guidance systems. An example of these are to be found in the Differential Aptitude Tests (DAT) which contain the Career Planning Questionnaire and the DET Career Planning Report. Another example is the program developed by the U.S. Employment Services. The core of the USES career counseling program is the Guide for Occupational Exploration, intended for use by both counselors and by test takers themselves. The Guide categorizes thousands of occupations by major interest areas and by ability patterns and other traits required for successful performance. A few of the twelve interest areas which are included are selling, scientific, humanitarian, and mechanical and sixty six work groups classified under the appropriate interest areas; specific jobs are in turn listed under each work group. Some programs have been developed completely as career explorations systems rather than incorporating previously available instruments. Another approach to career counseling provides a procedure for integrating available information from many sources in a comprehensive career exploration program.

Clinical Assessment

Question:
   37. Discuss clinical testing.

Answer:
In the intensive study of individual cases, Clinicians typically draw upon multiple sources of data. In order to build up an integrated picture of the individual, information is derived from interviewing and from the case history and is combined with the test scores. When an alert and trained clinician is in active contact with an individual during the hour or so required to administer a test, he or she can learn more about that person than is given by an IQ or some other single score. Besides using

intelligence tests to assess an individual's general level of intellectual functioning, clinical psychologists generally explore the pattern, or profile, of test scores for possible indices of psycho pathology. Other techniques and modifications having been recommended by several clinicians, specifically, any one of the major procedures having been utilized. The first of these involves the amount of scatter, or extent of variation among the individual's scores on all subtest. The second procedure is based upon the computation of a deterioration index based upon the difference between "hold" test, allegedly resistant to deterioration from pathology or old age and "don't hold" tests, considered to be susceptible to decline.

The third approach is based upon score patterns associated with particular clinical syndromes, such as brain damage, schizophrenia, anxiety state, and delinquency.

Question:
38. Briefly discuss the Bender Visual Motor Gestalt Test.

Answer:
The Bender Visual Motor Gestalt Test, more commonly known as the Bender Gestalt Test, is broadly used by clinical psychologists, basically for the detection of brain damage. In this test the nine simple designs are presented one at a time on cards. The respondent is instructed to copy each design, with the sample before her or him. These designs were selected by Bender from a longer series originally used by Wertheimer, who was one of the founders of the Gestalt school, in his studies of visual perception. The particular designs were constructed so as to show certain principles of Gestalt psychology. As screening instruments for detection of brain damage, the Benton test and the Bender-Gestalt have been proven to be among the most successful. In a survey of 94 studies using various instruments

with adult psychiatric patients, these tests offered a mid point percentage of correct classifications of about 75. This success rate includes both brain-damaged and non-brain damaged psychiatric cases that were correctly identified as such.

Question:
    39. Briefly discuss the behavior assessment procedure.

Answer:
The main functions to be served by assessment procedures in behavior therapy can be subsumed under three headings. First, assessment techniques help in defining the individual's problem through a functional analysis of relevant behavior. A second way in which assessment procedures can contribute to behavior therapy is in the selection of appropriate treatments. Thirdly, there is a need for assessing procedures which can in themselves be classified under three major types: self-report by the client, direct observation of behavior and physiological measures.

Some behavior assessment instruments have been evaluated by traditional statistical procedures and have met acceptable psychometric standards in retest, internal substance, and scorer reliability, as well as in several types of validation analyses. An example of this is the Social Performance Survey Schedule, self-report inventory designed to assess a wide variety of social behaviors while at the same time considerable attention is being given to the development of alternative statistical procedures that are appropriate for behavior assessment. These include single case research designs which an applicable to the clinical field as a whole and special ways of evaluating reliability and validity of measuring instruments designed specifically for behavior assessment.

Question:
    40. Discuss clinical judgment.

Answer:
This term "clinical" is usually used to refer to any methodology involving the intensive study of individual cases. A characteristic feature of clinical assessments is their reliance on judgment in at least some aspects of the process. The diagnostic role of the clinician can be described in terms of data gathering and data synthesis. By establishing and maintaining rapport, the clinician may elicit pertinent facts about his or her life history not readily accessible in other ways. Such life history data provides a particularly sound basis for understanding an individual and predicting subsequent behavior. Research on the process of clinical judgment has thrown considerable light on the relation between the data input and the clinician's output judgment, diagnosis, prediction. Correlation and regression analyses can indicate the relative contribution of different inputs to the final judgment and they can show whether the contribution is linear or is best represented by some nonlinear combination, as in the pattern or a configurable analysis or moderator variables.

Question:
41. Briefly discuss the Minnesota Multiphasic Personality Inventory.

Answer:
The Minnesota Multiphasic Personality Inventory is an example of criterion keying in personality test construction. Not only is the MMPI the most widely used personality inventory but it has also stimulated a flood of research. To date, over 8,000 references have been published about this test. The MMPI items consist of 550 affirmative statements to which the test taker gives a response "True", "False" or "Cannot Say". In the original, individual form of the test, the 550 items are printed in large type on separate cards, which the respondent sorts into the

three categories. In its original basic form, the MMPI provides scores on IQ "clinical scales".

- Hypochondria
- Depression
- Hysteria
- Psychopathic deviate
- Masculinity-femininity
- Paranoia
- Psychasthenia
- Schizophrenia
- Hypomania
- Social introversion

A special feature of MMPI is its utilization of three so-called validity scales. These scales are not concerned with validity in the technical sense. They represent checks on carelessness, misunderstanding, malingering, and the operation of special response sets and test-taking attitudes. The validating scores include: Lie score (L), Validity score (F), (a high F score may indicate scoring errors), Correction score (K), (this score provides a measure of test taking attitude). As an initial aid in the diagnostic interpretation of MMPI profiles, Hathaway and Meehl prepared an Atlas for the Clinical Use of the MMPI. This Atlas provides coded profiles and short case histories of 968 patients, arranged according to similarity of profile pattern. Computerized systems for completely automated profile interpretation is another step in the evolution of MMPI score interpretation.

Question:
  42. Discuss test-taking attitudes and response biases.

Answer:
Self-report inventories are especially subject to faking or malingering. Under other circumstances, respondents may be motivated to "fake bad" thereby making themselves appear more psychologically disturbed than they are. This may occur, for example, in the testing of persons on trial for a criminal offense. Many procedures have been followed in an effort to meet the problem of faking and related response sets in personality inventories. Construction of relatively "subtle" or socially neutral items may reduce the use of these factors in some inventories. In a number of situations, the test instructions and the establishment of rapport may motivate test takers to respond frankly, if they can be shown that by doing so it is more profitable to them. In certain situations, however, this may be ineffective and it would not have much effect on social desirability response sets of which the individual is unaware. Other attempted solutions include verification keys that detect faking or response tests, such as the F scale of the MMPI, and correction terms, such as those provided by the K scales of the MMPI. Still another procedure, directed not to the detection but to the prevention of dissimulation, is the use of forced choice items. This technique requires the respondent to choose between two descriptive terms or phrases that may both be desirable or both undesirable. In such cases, respondents must indicate which phrase is most characteristic and which is least characteristic of themselves. This item form has the advantage of yielding normative rather than positive scores and so imposing no artificial constraints on the interrelationships among different scales.

Question:
   43. Discuss the Study of Values.

Answer:
The Study of Values is a widely used and viable early instrument originally suggested by Spranger's Types of Men. This inventory was designed to measure the relative strength of six basic interests, motives, or evaluative attitudes. The six areas are theoretical, economic, aesthetic, social, political, and religious.

Items for the study of Values were first formulated on the basis of the theoretical framework provided by Spranger. Validity has been checked partly by the method of contrasted groups. Profiles of various educational and occupational samples exhibit significant differences in the expected directions. For example, medical students obtained their highest scores in the theoretical area, theological students in the religious area. Some relationships have been demonstrated between value profiles and academic achievement, especially when relative achievement in different fields is considered.

The Work Value Inventory was designed for use in academic or career counseling of high school and college students, as well as in personnel selection. This self-report inventory explores the scores of satisfaction one seeks in his/her work.

The Moral Judgment Scale describes six stages of moral development, ranging from a premoral level, through a morality of conventional conformity, to the formulation of self accepted moral principles derived by individual reasoning. He offers a cognitive model of moral development, based on the premise that individuals prefer the highest stage they can comprehend.

Question:
    44. Discuss Locus of Control.

Answer:
"Locus of Control" first came into prominence with the publication of a monograph by Rotter. In this publication Rotter presented the scale he has developed to assess the individual's generalized expectancies for internal versus external control of reinforcement. This instrument was constructed within the context of social-learning theory.

Internal control refers to the perception of an event as contingent upon one's own behavior or one's relatively permanent characteristics. External control, on the other hand, indicates that a positive or negative reinforcement following some action of the individual is perceived as not being entirely contingent upon his or her own action but the result of change, fate, or luck. Locus of control can itself be recognized as one aspect of a broader concept of casual attribution, which is receiving increasing attention from many investigators. The first locus of control in the more restricted sense, characterizes the cause as internal (aptitude, effort, health) or external (task difficulty, help from others, luck). A second dimension, stability, differentiates between more enduring causes, such as aptitude, and more changeable or modifiable causes, such as health, mood, and effort. A third dimension, controllability, differentiates on the basis of degree to which the condition is under the person's control.

Question:
45. Discuss Masculinity-Femininity (M-F) Scales.

Answer:
The pioneer instrument for measuring a psychological construct designated as masculinity-femininity (M-F) was developed by Terman and Miles. Essentially, items were selected empirically in terms of the relative frequency of each response given by

males and by females in the American culture of the time. "Attitude Interest Analysis" is the resulting inventory, and included seven subtests: Word Association, Inkblot Association, Information, Emotional and Ethical Attitudes, Interest, Personalities and Opinions, and Introvertive Response. The next two decades saw the development of several second-generation M-F scales. The best known examples are the M-F scales included in the MMPI, the California Psychological Inventory, and the Guilford-Zimmerman Temperament survey. Third generation M-F instruments appear in the 1970's. The principal examples are the Bem Sex-Role Inventory and the Personal Attributes Questionnaire developed by Spence and Helmreich. These third generation instruments differ in several major ways from the earlier instruments. First, the items are selected in terms of judges rating of their relative desirability for males or females and the degree to which they characterized each sex in our society. Therefore, what is assessed is the respondent's conformity to a currently accepted ideal or prevalent stereotype of male and female behavior. Second, masculinity and femininity are treated as independent and probably orthogonal variables; and persons high on both are classified as androgynous. Third, some efforts are being made to recognize multi-dimensionality through the empirical identification of item clusters and the consideration of situational influences.

Projectives

Question:
46. Briefly discuss inkblot techniques.

Answer:
The Rorschach inkblot is one of the most popular projective techniques. It was developed by the Swiss psychiatrist

Hermann Rorschach. Although standardized series of inkblots had previously been used by psychologists in studies of imagination and other functions, Rorschach was the first to apply inkblots to the diagnostic investigation of the personality as a whole. In the development of this method, Rorschach experimented with a large number of inkblots, which he administered to different psychiatric groups. As a result of such clinical observation, those response characteristics that differentiated between the various psychiatric syndromes were gradually incorporated into the scoring system. This scoring system was improved further by supplementary testing of mental retardates, normals, artists, scholars and other persons of known characteristics. Rorschach's method used 10 cards, on each is printed a bilaterally symmetrical inkblot. Five of the blots are executed in shades of gray and black only; two contain touches of bright red, and the remaining three contain several pastel shades. As the respondent is shown each inkblot, he or she is asked to tell what the blot could represent. A verbatim record of the responses, position or positions in which cards are held, spontaneous remarks, emotional expressions, and other incidental behavior of the respondent during the tests session is kept. While several systems for scoring and interpreting the Rorschach have been developed, the most common scoring categories include location, determinants and content. Location in this case refers to the part of the blot with which the respondent associates each response. The determinants of the response include form, color, shading, and movement. The treatment of content varies from one scoring system to another. The human figure, human details, animal figures, animal details, and anatomical diagrams are some of the major categories used.

Question:
47. Discuss Thematic Apperception Test (T.A.T.)

Answer:
Thematic Apperception Test presents more highly structured stimuli and requires more complex and meaningfully organized verbal responses. Interpretation of responses by the examiner is usually based on content analysis of a rather qualitative nature. T.A.T. has been widely used in clinical practice and research and has served as a model for the development of many other instruments. This test consists of nineteen cards containing vague pictures in black and white and one blank card. The respondent is asked to make up a story to fit each picture, telling what led up to the event shown in the picture, describing what is happening at the moment and what the characters are feeling and thinking and giving the outcome. The blank card is to be used for the respondent to imagine some picture on the card and to describe it and then tell a story about it. When interpreting T.A.T stories, the examiner first determines who is the "hero" the character of either sex with whom the respondent has presumably identified herself or himself. The content of the stories is then analyzed principally in reference to Murray's list of "need" and "press".

Question:
48. Present an evaluation of projective techniques.

Answer:
Some appear more promising than others because of more favorable experiential findings, sounder theoretical orientation, or both. Regarding some techniques, such as the Rorschach, extensive data has been gathered, though the interpretation is uncertain. Of the others, little is known, either because of their recent origin, or because objective fact is hindered by the essential nature of the instruments or by the attitudes of their exponents.

Most projective techniques represent an effective means for "breaking the ice" during the initial contacts between clinician and clients. The task is interesting and often entertaining. It diverts the individuals' attention away from himself or herself and so reduces embarrassment and defensiveness.

Most projective techniques are inadequately standardized with respect to both administration and scoring. Yet there is evidence that even subtle differences in the phrasing of verbal instructions and in examiner-examinee relationships can appreciably alter performance on these tests. Interpretation of projective test performance often involves subgroup norms, of either a subjective or an objective nature. So the clinician may have a general subjective picture of what constitutes a "typical" schizophrenic or brain damaged performance on a particular test.

For any test, the fundamental question is that of validity. Many validation studies of projective tests have been concerned with concurrent criterion-related validation. Most of these have compared the performance of entrusted groups, such as occupational or diagnostic groups. Still another common source of error, arising from reliance on clinical experience in the validation of diagnostic signs, is what Chapman labeled "illusory validation". This fact may account in part for the continued clinical use of instruments and systems of diagnostic signs for which empirical validity findings are predominantly negative.

Projective techniques are more and more being regarded as clinical tools. So they may serve as supplementary qualitative interviewing aids in the hands of a skilled clinician. Their value as clinical tools is proportional to the skill of the clinician and, therefore, cannot be assessed independently of the individual clinician using them. The nature of clinical judgment through which projective and interviewing data may be utilized in reaching decisions about individual cases is receiving increasing attention from psychologists. Such clinical predictions are helpful, provided they are not accepted as final but are constantly tested against information elicited through subsequent inquiry, test responses, reactions to therapy, or other behavior on the part of the client.

BRIEF PSYCHIATRIC RATING SCALE
J. E. Overall and D. R. Gorham

Directions: Place an X in the appropriate box to represent level of severity of each symptom.

PATIENT_____

RATER_____

NO._____

DATE_____

	Not Present	Very Mild	Mild	Moderate	Mod. Severe	Severe	Extremely Severe
1. SOMATIC CONCERN – preoccupation with physical health, fear of physical illness, hypochondriasis.	☐	☐	☐	☐	☐	☐	☐
2. ANXIETY – worry, fear, overconcern for present or future.	☐	☐	☐	☐	☐	☐	☐
3. EMOTIONAL WITHDRAWAL – lack of spontaneous interaction, isolation, deficiency in relating to others.	☐	☐	☐	☐	☐	☐	☐
4. CONCEPTUAL DISORGANIZATION – thought processes confused, disconnected, disorganized, disrupted.	☐	☐	☐	☐	☐	☐	☐
5. GUILT FEELINGS – self-blame, shame, remorse for past behavior.	☐	☐	☐	☐	☐	☐	☐
6. TENSION – physical and motor manifestations or nervousness, overactivation, tension.	☐	☐	☐	☐	☐	☐	☐
7. MANNERISMS AND POSTURE – peculiar, bizarre, unnatural motor behavior (not including tic).	☐	☐	☐	☐	☐	☐	☐

8. GRANDIOSITY – exaggerated self-opinion, arrogance, conviction of unusual power or abilities.	☐	☐	☐	☐	☐	☐	☐
9. DEPRESSIVE MOOD – sorrow, sadness, despondency, pessimism.	☐	☐	☐	☐	☐	☐	☐
10. HOSTILITY – animosity, contempt, belligerence, disdain for others.	☐	☐	☐	☐	☐	☐	☐
11. SUSPICIOUSNESS – mistrust, belief others harbor malicious or discriminatory intent.	☐	☐	☐	☐	☐	☐	☐
12. HALLUCINATORY BEHAVIOR – perceptions without normal external stimulus correspondence.	☐	☐	☐	☐	☐	☐	☐
13. MOTOR RETARDATION – slowed, weakened movements or speech; reduced body tone.	☐	☐	☐	☐	☐	☐	☐
14. UNCOOPERATIVENESS – resistance, guardedness, rejection of authority.	☐	☐	☐	☐	☐	☐	☐
15. UNUSUAL THOUGHT CONTENT – unusual, odd, strange, bizarre thought content.	☐	☐	☐	☐	☐	☐	☐
16. BLUNTED AFFECT – reduced emotional tone, reduction in normal intensity of feelings flatness.	☐	☐	☐	☐	☐	☐	☐
17. EXCITEMENT – heightened emotional tone, agitation, increased reactivity.	☐	☐	☐	☐	☐	☐	☐
18. DISORIENTATION – confusion or lack of proper association for person, place, or time.	☐	☐	☐	☐	☐	☐	☐

Drugs continued: _____ New Drugs:_____

www.ingramcontent.com/pod-product-compliance
Lightning Source LLC
Chambersburg PA
CBHW070800100426
42742CB00012B/2200